1940 1950 1960 1970 1980 1990

THE LEGEND OF
Dr Pepper/Seven-Up

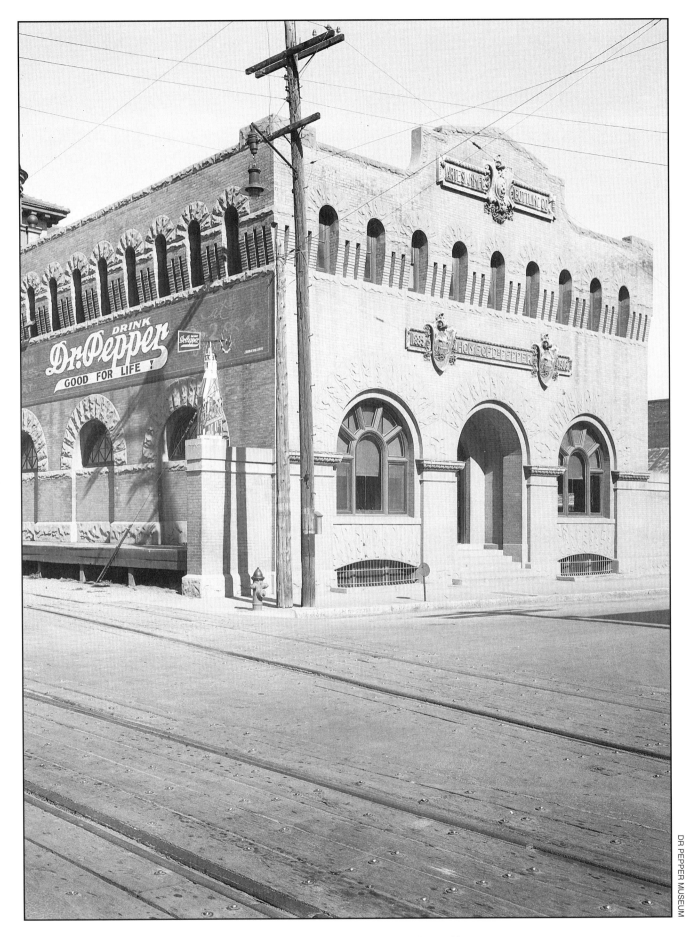

The original Dr Pepper bottling plant in Waco, Texas, today the home of the renowned Dr Pepper Museum.

THE LEGEND OF
Dr Pepper/Seven-Up

JEFFREY L. RODENGEN

Published by Write Stuff Syndicate, Inc.

For Kevin and Chloé
The effervescence in my life...

Also by Jeff Rodengen

The Legend of Chris-Craft
IRON FIST: *The Lives of Carl Kiekhaefer*
Evinrude-Johnson and The Legend of OMC
Serving The Silent Service: The Legend of Electric Boat
The Legend of Honeywell
The Legend of Ingersoll-Rand
The Legend of Briggs & Stratton
The Legend of The Stanley Works

Copyright © 1995 by Write Stuff Syndicate, Inc. All rights reserved. No part of this book may be reproduced or transmitted in any form by any means, electronic or mechanical, including photocopying and recording, or by any information storage or retrieval system, without permission in writing from the publisher.

Write Stuff Syndicate, Inc.

1323 S.E. 17th Street, Suite 421
Ft. Lauderdale FL 33316-9958
1-800-900-Book
(1-800-900-2665)
(305) 462-6657

Library of Congress Catalog Card Number
95-060796

ISBN 0-945903-49-9

Completely produced in the United States of America

10 9 8 7 6 5 4 3 2 1

Table of Contents

Introduction		vi
Foreword	By Dave Thomas, Founder, Wendy's International	viii
Acknowledgements		x
Chapter I	The Birthplace of Dr Pepper	12
Chapter II	The Old Corner Drug Store	20
Chapter III	The Dr Pepper Company	28
Chapter IV	Ten, Two and Four	40
Chapter V	In a Class by Itself	52
Chapter VI	Going National	64
Chapter VII	The Founding of Seven-Up	78
Chapter VIII	The Thirties	84
Chapter IX	The H.C. Grigg Years	90
Chapter X	The Uncola	100
Chapter XI	Merging Dr Pepper and Seven-Up	108
Chapter XII	Cadbury Schweppes	118
Notes to Sources		130
Index		136

Introduction

IT ALL BEGAN in 1885, behind the counter of a popular drug store in rough-and-tumble Waco, Texas. Working at the soda fountain, Charles Alderton mixed together a distinctive combination of flavors, creating a new drink that became an instant success. First known only as a "Waco," it was later named Dr Pepper by his boss, Wade Morrison, who had once worked for a Virginia physician named Charles Pepper. (The period in the title was dropped twice, once in the early part of the century and then permanently in 1953.)

Morrison joined entrepreneur Robert Lazenby to bottle and promote the new drink, and Dr Pepper grew to be a successful, though regional, favorite. Lazenby's son-in-law, John Bernard O'Hara, president of the company from 1933 to 1944, tirelessly promoted his belief that Dr Pepper was "liquid food" that should be consumed at 10 a.m., 2 p.m. and 4 p.m. to fight fatigue.

In the late Sixties, an enterprising salesman with the improbable name of Woodrow Wilson "Foots" Clements rose to the position of president and CEO. Clements realized that a good portion of the nation was deprived of the unique flavor of Dr Pepper, and he worked methodically to spread the word. By the time he left the presidency to become full-time chairman in 1980, Dr Pepper was

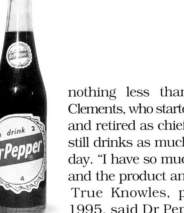

nothing less than a national sensation. Clements, who started selling Dr Pepper in 1935 and retired as chief executive officer in 1986, still drinks as much as a case of Dr Pepper a day. "I have so much feeling for the company and the product and the people," he said.

True Knowles, president from 1990 to 1995, said Dr Pepper only recently began realizing its potential. "Dr Pepper really is 109 years old, but it's really only been a national brand since 1970 and it's only had national exposure in the last five years. So if you think about it, it's a very, very young and new brand in most parts of the country."

In the early Eighties, Dr Pepper acquired Canada Dry and Welch's before entering a dizzying era of leveraged buy-outs and mergers. In 1986, after divesting Canada Dry, the company merged with Seven-Up, another leader in the fast-growing non-cola category, acquiring IBC Root Beer at the same time. Jim Ball, vice president of corporate communications, remembers that enthusiasm was high. "We could have the No. 1 and No. 2 non-cola brands with the best combination of bottlers," he recalled.

Seven-Up began life with the unlikely name of Bib-Label Lithiated Lemon-Lime Soda. Formulated by Charles L. Grigg of St. Louis in 1929, it was first sold in distinctive, 7-ounce, brown-tinted bottles. Later the bottles were tinted green. Grigg's son, Ham, became president in 1940, and remained at the helm of the company for 25 years.

Besides its delightful flavor, 7UP was promoted as a cure-all for such maladies as overwork, mental lassitude, over-worry and over-smoking. When Prohibition was repealed in 1933, sales of 7UP grew as its popularity as a mixer became widely known. There are few bars on Earth today that don't mix a "7 and 7," a combination of 7UP and Seagram's 7.

In 1967, Seven-Up launched the highly successful Uncola campaign. "I'd be a liar if I didn't tell you my first reaction was that it doesn't make sense," said William E. Winter, vice president of Seven-Up marketing at the time. But the Uncola campaign brilliantly positioned Seven-Up as a unique-tasting alternative to colas.

In 1978, the Seven-Up Company was purchased by Philip Morris, Inc., the powerful company that had made Miller Beer and Marlboro cigarettes industry leaders. But Philip Morris mistakenly believed that selling Seven-Up was just like selling beer, and the soft drink brand began losing money. In 1986, Philip Morris sold the international portion of the business to Pepsico Inc., and the national portion was merged with Dr Pepper.

The soft drink business is a high-stakes, highly competitive industry, with products constantly being introduced, marketed, packaged and distributed. The taste of the drink, though critically important, is only a fraction of the delicate formula for success. Soft drink companies must invest millions of dollars launching and promoting beverages, while relying on a unique bottling system that places responsibility for brand success in the hands of independent bottling franchises that package, market and distribute the product in their own protected territories.

Both Dr Pepper and Seven-Up survived Prohibition, the Great Depression, two world wars, and the leveraged buyouts and frenzied financial transactions of the Eighties. They each pioneered unique and creative ways to package and promote their products, from vending machines and cans to innovative plastic bottles. They introduced successful diet versions of their products, and changed the formulas of their diet brands when the Food and Drug Administration banned cyclamates in 1969. They fine-tuned their market positioning along with their logos, and gambled millions of dollars on memorable marketing campaigns.

On March 2, 1995, Cadbury Beverages, the beverage division of Cadbury Schweppes plc, purchased the Dr Pepper/Seven-Up Companies for $1.7 billion, fulfilling its goal of becoming the largest non-cola soft drink company in the world. The combined company, with such well-known brands as A&W, Hires, Mott's, Welch's, Canada Dry, Schweppes and Sunkist, commands more than half of the United States' non-cola market, and 17 percent of the total soft drink market. It's the third-largest soft drink company in the world, behind Coke and Pepsi. "One company has never owned so many brands," said John Brock, president of Cadbury Beverages North America.

Schweppes, founded by Jean Jacob Schweppe in 1783, and Cadbury, the renowned chocolate and candy manufacturer founded in 1824 by John Cadbury, merged in 1969. Cadbury Schweppes has expanded steadily over the ensuing 25 years, and now sells soft drinks and candy in more than 190 countries, and employs 40,000 people worldwide.

With a phenomenal mix of popular brands and an enviable worldwide distribution network, Dr Pepper and 7UP, along with the entire Cadbury Schweppes organization, are poised for spectacular growth. The stories of how these internationally recognized brands were created, and how they prospered against seemingly unsurmountable odds, are surprising and inspirational.

FOREWORD

by

Dave Thomas
Founder, Wendy's International

I FIRST MET W.W. "Foots" Clements, the retired chairman of Dr Pepper, over 20 years ago. I had opened the first Wendy's on November 15th, 1969 in Columbus, Ohio, and I put Dr Pepper on the menu from the beginning. I had first tried Dr Pepper in Texas—where it's the No. 1 drink—and I knew it was the right thing to do. I liked it, and I thought it'd be something different.

Another thing attracted me to Dr Pepper, the fact that both Wendy's and Dr Pepper were *quality* products. Also, Foots Clements and I both came from a similar background—I was a short order cook, and he was a truck driver. He worked hard and rose to the top of the company. I just think he's a super guy.

Some readers may know that I was adopted when I was 6 weeks old. My adoptive parents moved from Atlantic City to Michigan, where my mother died when I was 5. My foster dad moved on to Indiana, then Tennessee, and then back to Indiana. I've been on my own since I was 15. If there is one thing all children deserve, it's a loving family. They deserve the love, attention and guidance of a nurturing mother and father. But it doesn't always work that way. Thousands of children of all ages, throughout this country, don't have a permanent family — and they're looking for help. One way you can help is by considering adoption. Please contact your local adoption group or agency to learn how you can become adoptive parents.

When I was 12 years old in Knoxville, I got a job working the counter at the Regas Restaurant. We weren't allowed to use serving trays, so I had to learn how to balance plates, cups and saucers, and carry everything by hand. The big challenge was to carry four plates of food and multiple cups of coffee at the same time without dripping or spilling anything. If you could do that, you were a success. Also all orders were taken by memory, and checks were made out the same way. We often had a hundred customers in a single night.

During the summer, I worked at the Regas every day. During the school year, I worked every weekend. The Regas was open 24 hours a day, and I worked the 12-hour shift from 8 p.m. to 8 a.m. We would start cleaning up at 2 a.m., and then we'd make egg, ham and tuna sandwiches for the next day. Sometimes we'd make up as many as 400 sandwiches a night. This was during World War II, and everybody working back home tried to give a little extra on the job.

Breakfast service began at 4 a.m. After making sandwiches, I would work until 8 in the morning, go home, fall into bed and sleep until about 3 in the afternoon. This work style set a standard for me. I became used to putting out a lot of volume when I was very young. I just thought that it was the way you were supposed to do it. If somebody pays you, it was up to you to perform.

The history of both Dr Pepper and Seven-Up is filled with the hard work and self-sacrifice of its executives and employees, and it's safe to say that neither brand would be the success it is without this kind of dedication. I also think that it's more of a personalized, family-oriented company. I found that particularly true when Foots was the CEO. They have always given Wendy's great service or we wouldn't use them and their products.

PepsiCo Inc. is now the largest restauranteur in the world, with their ownership of Kentucky Fried Chicken, Pizza Hut and Taco Bell, and a direct competitor to Wendy's. We have over 4,000 restaurants now, but I think Pepsi Co has an ad that says they're building a store every four hours or something. So they take the food dollar away from us. They try to. We try to take it away from them, too.

Many people ask me how I view the future of the fast-food industry, and I think the changes are going to be particularly in the area of nutrition, lower fats and lower calories. I think that nutrition is going to be a big part of our life and I think the soft drink industry will change, too. More diet drinks, and better-tasting diet drinks. Taking the industry as a whole, I don't think that diet drinks are the best tasting. I would think that Dr Pepper with the taste that they have, and Seven-Up could be the leaders in that role. That's their big opportunity.

Dr Pepper, Seven-Up and Wendy's have all succeeded because they started with the basics: quality, service and taste. If you can master those elements over the years, the way Dr Pepper and Seven-up have, you can't help but grow. I'm glad to see both brands growing at over twice the rate of the rest of the industry. It tells me that quality and uniqueness still have a chance. Remember, you're hearing this from someone who makes square hamburgers.

ACKNOWLEDGEMENTS

MANY PEOPLE and institutions assisted in the research, preparation and publication of *The Legend of Dr Pepper/Seven-Up*. The research, however, much less the book itself, would have been impossible without the dedicated assistance of Dr Pepper/Seven-Up executives, employees and retirees. Principal among these is James A. Ball III — senior vice president of corporate communications, whose courteous and affable guidance made it possible to locate and identify both prominent records and individuals crucial to the Dr Pepper/Seven-Up legacy.

Instrumental to our research team were the critical insights made available by former Dr Pepper/Seven-Up Companies Chairman John R. Albers; former Executive Vice President and Chief Financial Officer Ira Rosenstein; former Dr Pepper President True H. Knowles; former Seven-Up President Francis I. Mullin III, Premier Beverages Vice President Mike McGrath; recently retired Senior Vice President of Operations Charles P. Grier; former Dr Pepper Chairman W.W. "Foots" Clements, and former Seven-Up Chairman William E. Winter.

A very special mention must be made of the pioneering research accomplished by others, particularly Harry E. Ellis and Daniel J. Forrestal, both deceased. Harry Ellis, former historian for the Dr Pepper Company, was hired in 1931, and was responsible for publishing the company magazine, *News and Views*, which changed its name to *ClockDial* in 1948. Ellis wrote a detailed history of Dr Pepper in 1979, called *Dr Pepper, King of Beverages*, and an update with the same title for the company's centennial in 1985, both of which were invaluable resources in the compiling of this work.

Detailed information on the history of the Seven-Up Company would not have been possible without the work of Forrestal, a former director of public relations at the Monsanto Company in St. Louis. Starting in 1977, Forrestal painstakingly researched and drafted a manuscript on the history of Seven-Up. Seven-Up and Forrestal intended to publish the history in 1979, but when Seven-Up was purchased by the Philip Morris Company in 1978, the project was unfortunately discontinued. His many insights into the fascinating historical legacy of Seven-Up are published here for the first time.

The author would like to thank the invaluable assistance afforded the project by the Cadbury Schweppes organization, both in London and in Stamford, Connecticut, with a special thanks to Chairman Dominic Cadbury, Cadbury Beverages Stream Managing Director Frank Swan and Dr Pepper/Cadbury North America President John Brock. Also assisting whenever help was needed were Chris Milburn, Catherine Lincoln, Dora McCabe and Jennifer Andrews in London, and Kathy Healey and Catherine Van Evans in Stamford, among others.

Every historical research project needs an ultimate authority upon which the team can rely for double-checking the accuracy of their work. In the case of *The Legend of Dr Pepper/*

Seven-Up, the author and his staff relied heavily on the courtesy, generosity and knowledge of Mildred G. "Milly" Walker, curator of collections at the Dr Pepper Museum in Waco, Texas. Both Milly and Museum Director Joe Cavanaugh's boundless enthusiasm for the history of the soft drink industry has resulted in a world-class museum whose scope encompasses the entire universe of soft drink companies, both past and present. The author can sincerely recommend and advise those who have private archives and artifacts from the soft drink industry to consider both archival and financial donations or bequests to this exceptional institution.

Many readers may be unaware of the great contribution that a skillful and resourceful editor can make for a historical biography such as *The Legend of Dr Pepper/Seven-Up*. Write Stuff Syndicate, Inc. Executive Editor Karen Nitkin's imaginative and thoughtful editing and draft coordination have made the difference between a catalog of historical data and an enjoyable literary experience.

The development of historical time-lines and a portion of the principal archival research were accomplished by the author's Dallas-based research assistant, Bailey Hankins. His research into, and editing of previously published works have made it possible to provide consolidated information on the origins and evolution of this unique organization.

Also helping whenever needed were Maribeth Exley of the Dr Pepper/Seven-Up Companies corporate communications department; Pat Bowen, administrative assistant to W.W. "Foots" Clements; Pat Hupp, administrative assistant to Charles P. Grier in St. Louis; Carol Smith; Cala Thomas; Corporate Attorney Kim Yee; Paparazzi Photography Studio in Dallas — especially photographers Brad Chrisenberry and Jeff Laydon; the staff at Citijet at Dallas Love Field; Mark Kloster; Diane Kloster; Seth Turner; Linda Carlisle for locating a valuable living legacy; the Baylor University Institute for Oral History, for the oral memoirs of Clements, a series of interviews conducted by Thomas Lee Charlton and David B. Stricklin from May 9, 1984 through September 8, 1986; Dollie Cole—the Dr Pepper Girl—for loaning us her irreplaceable photos; and especially R. David "Dave" Thomas, foreword contributor, sensitive humanitarian, author of *Dave's Way* and *Well Done! The Common Guy's Guide to Everyday Success*, and founder of Wendy's International.

The interest and courtesy of the many interview subjects for the book were most gratifying, and the author would like to thank Senior Vice President Corporate Communications James A. Ball III; Senior Vice President of Marketing for Dr Pepper John Clarke; James Gwaltney, Ph.D.; bottlers Edmund Hoffman, Jim Turner, Bill Kloster, James C. "Jimmy" Lee, Jr.; Robert Quirk, former senior vice president of sales for Seven-Up USA; and James H. Wade, Ph.D., vice president manufacturing, Waco Manufacturing Company; among others.

Finally, a very special thanks to the dedicated staff at Write Stuff Syndicate, Inc., especially Executive Assistant and Office Manager Bonnie Bratton; Creative Director, graphic illustrator and cover artist Kyle Newton; Project Analyst Karine N. Rodengen; Graphic Designer Anne Boeckh and Logistics Specialist Joe Kenny.

This beautiful lithograph promoted Dr Pepper in 1905. "The Year Round" slogan was used only between 1900 and 1906.

CHAPTER I
THE BIRTHPLACE OF DR PEPPER

"At 5 o'clock this afternoon, the recent trouble between J.W. Harris and G.B. Gerald culminated in a shooting affray at the corner of Fourth and Austin streets, in which J.W. Harris was mortally wounded, W.A. Harris was killed and G.B. Gerald was shot in two places. J.W. Harris was standing at the Old Corner Drug Store."

— Waco Daily Telephone, November 19, 1897

WACO IN THE LATE 1880s was a dusty town with a colorful assortment of saloons and hotels. Most residents were ordinary citizens struggling to pry a living out of the land and leave the devastation of the Civil War behind. But this brawling prairie village on the fringe of the Texas hill country was also host to some of the most famous and feared characters in Western history.

Waco began as an Indian settlement on the west bank of the Brazos River. In 1837, a company of Texas Rangers, led by Major George Erath, established a fort, and white settlers soon gathered in the surrounding area. The town was officially incorporated in 1857, but significant growth was delayed by the Civil War.[1] In January 1870, the largest suspension bridge in the United States was built across the Brazos River.

From the beginning, Waco exhibited what can only be described as a split personality. In his book *Brann the Iconoclast*, Charles Carver notes the town's two primary nicknames in the 1880s and 1890s: "The Athens of Texas" and "Six-Shooter Depot." Both were accurate.[2] The same town that encouraged art and supported four separate schools of advanced learning frequently echoed with the sound of gunfire.

For most of America, the 1880s was a time of growth and healing after the agony of the Civil War. Before the decade was out, streets and buildings would be lit by electricity, and the nation's first skyscraper would loom 10 stories over Chicago. But cities and towns in the South and West were only slightly affected by the changes and discoveries profoundly altering the North.

Entertainment, Waco-Style

Outlaws flocked to Waco for its recreational opportunities, gambling and drinking in its numerous saloons, and enjoying the company of prostitutes in quasi-legal brothels. The town leaders realized they could not eliminate prostitution, so they decided to control it by setting up a red light district. By 1890, Waco had the dubious distinction of having Texas' first, and America's second, licensed reservation for prostitutes. These women were licensed annually "to occupy or reside in a bawdy house or pursue the occupation of bawd." Madams paid the city $10 a year for each bedroom, plus $10 for each "bawd or inmate." They also paid $2 for exams required every two weeks to maintain a health certificate. Though prostitution was considered immoral, the Waco system proved so effective at preventing venereal disease that it survived until 1913.

As Waco grew and developed, its frontier spirit was exhibited in barroom brawls, gunfights and random shootings. One such incident is related to the history of Dr Pepper. In the fall of 1858, shortly after Waco was incorporated, a gunfighter named Long swaggered into town. According to witnesses, he hadn't been in town more than a few days before he began insulting businessman Henry Lazenby's family. Lazenby apparently took the slander quite seriously. He waited outside

Waco had a split personality at the end of the 19th Century. As a center of education and commerce, it was known as "The Athens of Texas," but frequent gunfights within the city limits also earned it the nickname "Six-Shooter Depot."

Waco's famous suspension bridge, 475 feet long, spans the Brazos River. A remarkable architectural achievement for 1870, the bridge brought many travelers through Waco on their way to new homes in the West.

Oakes' drugstore, and when Long appeared, Lazenby "gave him notice" and fired one shot, killing him instantly. Since Lazenby had warned Long, he was acquitted in a trial that was little more than a formality. Lazenby would be very important in the early days of Dr Pepper. His brother Robert would be one of the company founders, and Henry would manage the Artesia Bottling Company of Fort Worth, Texas.

The Train Crash at Crush

On September 15, 1896, an unusual event took place in the fictional town of Crush, 16 miles north of Waco. An employee of the Missouri-Kansas-Texas Railroad, known as the Katy, arranged for two locomotives to crash head-on. The idea had occurred to Bill Crush when his train's boiler exploded on a trip from St. Louis. The wreck attracted thousands of spectators, and Crush reasoned that another crash, publicized in advance, would generate publicity for the railroad all over the country. Crush managed to talk Katy officials into his plan, and 14 special-excursion trains carried passengers paying $2 apiece for round-trip tickets to witness the collision. People poured into the Waco area from every part of the country, and on the big day more than 40,000 spectators were on hand.[3]

Two 35-ton locomotives, each pulling six empty box cars, backed a mile away from the site. The suspense mounted as the boilers of both trains were stoked to achieve maximum speed. Then, at 5 p.m., the trains roared down the tracks. The engineers pushed the trains to maximum speed, and then jumped off. When the trains collided, both were going at least 60 miles per hour. Crush later swore that experts had assured him neither locomotive's boiler would explode. But both burst on collision. An earth-shaking roar rolled for miles across the prairie, stampeding cattle and terrifying wildlife. The air was filled with thousands of red-hot scraps of metal. The crowd had pressed close to the tracks, and at least three people were killed and scores were injured. When the smoke and dust finally cleared, stunned observers saw an incredible sight. The trains were fused together in a single mass of twisted steel, telescoped into a hissing and smoldering heap.[4]

The Judge vs. the Editor

By the late 1890s, the most notorious outlaws were either dead or languishing in prison. But citizens who were content to leave behind Waco's gun-fighting days were jolted on November 19, 1897. On that day, on the front steps of a drugstore near the city's main intersection, a feud between a local judge and two newspapermen erupted into a gunfight.

The trouble began with a newspaper article written by William Cowper Brann, known to his readers as the Iconoclast. In addition to a brilliant mind and stinging wit, Brann had a deep contempt for Baptists, clergymen of all persuasions, Englishmen, blacks and women. He created addi-

One of the earliest Dr Pepper signs is seen in 1897 on the front of the combination post office and grocery store in the tiny settlement of Richie, Texas.

In a bizarre publicity stunt, Katy Railroad employee Bill Crush arranged for two locomotives traveling at full speed to crash head-on. More than 40,000 thrill-seekers attended the spectacle, and at least three were killed when the colliding trains showered red-hot scraps of metal on the crowd.

tional enemies with each new article. Within three years of his arrival in Waco, Brann's articles had divided the town into armed camps.[5]

One of Brann's staunchest supporters was Judge G.B. Gerald, a Confederate war hero who had been seriously wounded four times. At the Battle of Gettysburg, where he commanded a regiment of infantry, he had been nearly killed and was left with a crippled left arm. At 62, the judge enjoyed a reputation as a fighter and a man of fierce honor. He admired Brann's intellect and courage in attacking what he considered hypocrisy in high places.

An uneasy truce existed between Brann's friends and his enemies until the day he launched a bitter attack on the Baptist Baylor University in

Waco. In a particularly vicious article, Brann cast aspersions on the collective intelligence of the university's faculty and the sexual morality of the female students. The attack infuriated Waco's predominantly Baptist population.[6]

At this point, Judge Gerald jumped into the fray, penning a long letter defending Brann and delivered it personally to J.W. Harris, editor of the *Waco Times Herald*. Unfortunately for the judge, Harris was a devout Baptist who was not interested in publishing a defense of Brann. He grudgingly accepted the letter, but showed no inclination to publish it. When Gerald finally lost patience and appeared at the editor's office to reclaim the document, Harris refused to hand it over.[7]

This vexation was too much for the judge. According to a bulletin he later posted around town, the disagreement turned violent.

Judge G.B. Gerald was both feared and respected in Waco. When newspaper editor Jim Harris refused to publish or return his letter, Gerald challenged him to a duel.

Before he could complete his draw, the newsman was on him again, and the judge's weapon clattered to the floor. He tumbled head-first down a flight of stairs.[9]

The next day, the judge circulated yellow handbills describing his encounter with Harris. Referring to the editor as "a liar, a coward and a cur," Gerald offered to settle their differences "in the traditional manner of gentlemen."[10] Harris declined, but he bought a high-quality revolver and began practicing daily. His brother, Bill Harris, also purchased a pistol, and was improving his own marksmanship.[11] A showdown was inevitable. On November 19, the judge drove his buggy into town and hitched it in front of the Old Corner Drug Store, one of Waco's most prominent gathering spots. Jim Harris was lounging in the doorway, and his brother was across the street, near the Citizens' National Bank. As Judge Gerald started for the door, Jim Harris fired but missed. Gerald drew and fired, striking Jim Harris in the throat. Harris dropped his pistol and fell back into the drugstore, unconscious and mortally wounded.[12]

"Provoked beyond endurance, I at last told him — knowing I was physically unable to engage in a fisticuff with him — to get his pistol, come out into the street, and we would make it a matter of life or death. He refused to do it. I then left. He followed me up through the hallway to the stairway, still continuing to talk over the matter, still refusing to give what was unquestionably mine, and at last waited until he got me in a position where, even if my physical strength had been equal to his, he would have had a great advantage over me. By his own acts and by his own conduct, he provoked me into saying words that he of course used to justify himself in striking me. When he delivered the first blow — and I believe he had some foreign substance in his hand — I felt my eye closed from the blood rushing from the gash above my eyebrow."[8]

Bleeding from the wound over his eye, Gerald reached for a pistol in his waistband.

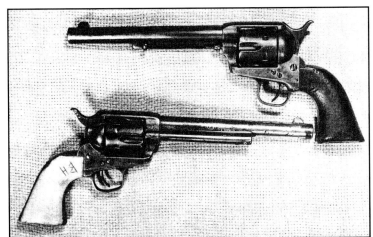

These Colt Peacemakers were used by the Harris brothers.

The Old Corner Drug Store, famous as the birthplace of Dr Pepper, anchored the busy intersection of Fourth and Austin avenues in downtown Waco. A gunfight here left two prominent citizens dead and one permanently disabled.

While Gerald was occupied with Jim Harris, Bill Harris ran into the street and fired three times at his back. Two of the shots found their mark. The judge, his face twisted in pain and fury, snarled, "This rotten bastard shot me in the back." He thrust his pistol against Bill Harris' forehead and pulled the trigger. The fight was over.[13]

Showing no signs of distress, Judge Gerald straightened his shoulders and walked across the street to the office of Dr. N.A. Olive in the First National Bank Building. The doctor administered a light anesthetic and amputated the judge's mangled left arm. Awakening a few minutes later, Gerald asked for a cigar, then inquired of a friend, "Where did I hit Jim Harris?" The friend replied, "Right in the Adam's apple, Judge." The judge shook his head and said, "Well, I guess that's not too bad. I was aiming at the son of a bitch's collar button."[14] The next day, the incident was reported in a special edition of the *Waco Daily Telephone*.

"At a time when the streets of Waco were crowded with men, women and children, this afternoon, a street duel occurred on the most prominent business corner of this city, during which many shots were exchanged.

"It is one of the most deplorable tragedies that has ever occurred. All bystanders and pedestrians escaped injury, with one exception, as the shooting seemed to be indiscriminate and occurred at a time when the streets were thronged."[15]

Five months later, on April 1, 1898, William Brann himself was killed on a Waco street by a Baylor sympathizer named Tom Davis. Before he died, Brann fatally wounded Davis. A local policeman, unaware of Brann's injuries, walked him a block and a half to the city jail before noticing his boots were full of blood. The crusty old journalist died shortly thereafter.

Judge G.B. Gerald died in 1914 at the age of 79. In a 1962 magazine article, Texas writer Roger Conger described him as "one of the last of the real old Confederate fire eaters."[16]

The Old Corner Drug Store

The Old Corner Drug Store, scene of this deadly gunfight, ultimately became famous for an entirely different reason. It was here, in 1885, that a young pharmacist named Charles C. Alderton devised the formula for Dr Pepper. He would have been astonished if he had foreseen the impact his discovery would have on Waco and its citizens, and upon other towns and other people throughout the world.

Even before the turn of the 20th Century, Dr Pepper advertising lithographs stressed a wholesome, refreshing image. Note the unique opener, made of brass wire, on the table.

Chapter II
The Old Corner Drug Store

"The popularity of the new drink was such that soda fountain owners from the surrounding territory purchased the syrup that Mr. Morrison had already named Dr Pepper."

— William McCullough

In 1880, a Waco pharmacist named John W. Castles opened a drugstore at the northeast corner of Fourth and Austin, one of the town's busiest intersections. Two years later, he took pharmacist W.B. Morrison as his partner, and the establishment became Castles and Morrison Drug Store. Born in Virginia in 1852, Morrison worked as a pharmacist in Austin and Round Rock, Texas, before moving to Waco.

Before long, Morrison bought out Castles, changing the name of the enterprise to Morrison's Old Corner Drug Store.[1] Waco was growing fast, and the drug store was growing apace. The Old Corner Drug Store was so successful that in 1911, it moved to larger quarters next to the Amicable Building, Waco's first skyscraper and the tallest building west of the Mississippi at the time.

Drugstores in the mid-1800s were often operated by physicians who sold prescriptions and soap out front, and repaired gunshot wounds and other ailments in the back. A variety of patent medicines were always for sale, including Dr. John Bull's Worm Destroyer, Ma Sutter's Celebrated Stomach Bitters and Benedict's Balm of Childhood. Alcohol was the primary ingredient, with cocaine, laudanum and other drugs often thrown in for added effect. Some of these patent medicines contained a higher proof than whiskey.

The Old Corner Drug Store was a popular meeting place. Some patrons wore boots and cowboy hats, while others favored Eastern-style fedoras and string ties. Inside was a slate where patients could leave medical questions and messages for their physicians, and a metal post in the store's recessed entrance was used to post other messages.[2]

One of Morrison's employees was Charles C. Alderton, a young pharmacist who also dispensed soft drinks and confections at the soda fountain. Alderton, born in New York in 1857, went to school in England. This background may have played a part in his interest in carbonated beverages, since the English were leaders in the research and development of carbonation.[3] Although Alderton earned his medical degree at the University of Texas in Galveston, he decided to make pharmacy his life work. In 1854, he married Lillie E. Walker of Galveston, Texas, and took her to Waco, where he secured a job in Morrison's Old Corner Drug Store.

A Unique Creation

In addition to his duties as a pharmacist, Alderton worked at the soda fountain, a popular attraction at Morrison's drug store. Carbonated water, a relatively new invention, was a popular refreshment, especially when flavored with fruit syrups. The most popular drink at the drug store was sarsaparilla, a beverage made with the dried roots of the sarsaparilla plant. Other drinks could be created on demand from formulas in the pharmacists' little black books. All made exaggerated claims about their health benefits, a practice that would later be continued by Dr Pepper.

Alderton's creation of Dr Pepper was recounted by William H. McCullough, who, in 1896, became secretary and treasurer of the company that sold Dr Pepper. McCullough, who worked closely with the founders of Dr Pepper, wrote the account in the late Thirties or early Forties.

> *"He experimented with different flavors and ingredients at odd times and being pleased with the palatability of the mixture that later was to be named Dr Pepper, he submitted it to Mr. Morrison."*[4]

Although the exact date when Alderton first poured the unique blend is unknown, the U.S. Patent Office recognizes December 1, 1885 as the official date when Dr Pepper was first served at the Old Corner Drug Store.[5]

Alderton's new taste treat quickly became a favorite. Since it had no official name, patrons would ask for a "Waco," or tell the soda jerk to "Shoot a Waco."[6]

Naming the New Drink

The new drink became so popular that Alderton could no longer postpone the task of giving it a name. At the time, it was common to give products names preceded by *Dr.*, in hopes of making them sound healthful. Patents awarded in 1885 included Dr. Davis' Liver Pills, Dr. Bell's Never-Failing Wonderful Mixture for Chills and Fevers, Dr. Chandler's Hemlock Plaster, and Dr. Able's Compound Honey of Tar and Lemon. Since carbonated beverages were considered healthful, it made sense to give them names that sounded medicinal.[7]

The creators of Dr Pepper followed this trend, though further inspiration apparently came from Morrison, who had worked in a drug store owned by physician Charles T. Pepper before moving to

Interior of the Old Corner Drug Store, a popular meeting place in Waco. Patrons sitting at the fountain would ask the soda jerk to "Shoot a Waco" when they wanted the popular new drink later known as Dr Pepper.

DR PEPPER MUSEUM

DR PEPPER MUSEUM

Texas. The physician had a young daughter, and according to the McCullough account, the drink was named in honor of her.

"In the presence of stockholders, [Morrison] smilingly remarked that when he was a young man and was living at Wytheville, Virginia, he was very much in love with a Miss Pepper whose father was a physician there. He gave the beverage the name because of his admiration for the young lady."[8]

Though this version of events was promoted through the years, there is strong reason to believe it is not true. Charles Pepper's great granddaughter, Jean Gillepsie Walker, noted in a 1982 letter that Pepper's daughter was only 8 when Morrison went to Texas.

"Our family has always understood the story of the naming of the beverage to be as reported, except that it happened in Bristol, Tennessee, where he practiced before moving to Rural Retreat in 1879. [Dr Pepper] had three sons and two daughters. One daughter died at age 3, the other, Ruth, married my grandfather, Barnes Gillepsie of Tazewell. She was not born until 1874 so I doubt the romantic element."[9]

Other stories of the naming of Dr Pepper have been accepted over the years. According to an

Above left:
Wade B. Morrison, owner of the Old Corner Drug Store, where Dr Pepper was invented. Morrison helped refine and promote the new drink.

Above right:
Charles Courtice Alderton, the pharmacist credited with inventing the drink.

PAPARAZZI PHOTOGRAPHY STUDIO—DR PEPPER/SEVEN-UP

anecdotal history of the Pepper family by Florence Pepper Raya, it was one of Charles Pepper's three sons, Louis Ervin Pepper, who created the drink.

> *"He was 'Dr Pepper.' One day he fixed up a formula in his father's drug store for a new drink. A young man who worked in the drug store left and went to Waco, Texas, where he worked in a drug store there. He knew the formula for the new drink and fixed up some, telling his friends he would like to put it on the market. One of the young men, sipping the new drink, said, 'Why not, and why not call the drink Dr Pepper?' That is the origin of the popular Dr Pepper soft drink of today."*[10]

Over the years, other stories were told. "Dr. Morrison himself told at least three different versions," said Milly Walker, curator of collections at the Dr Pepper Museum.[11] Walker, a highly respected historian, insists that the romantic element of the story is not true, and she is eager to set the record straight.

No matter what story is true, Charles Taylor Pepper has the unusual distinction of being immortalized by a soft drink. He was the 12th child of John Pepper and Mary Robertson Pepper

Dr. Charles Taylor Pepper probably never knew that his name was immortalized as a soft drink.

Dr. Pepper opened this drugstore in Rural Retreat, Virginia, just after the Civil War. It went out of business in 1994.

Chapter II: The Old Corner Drug Store

DR PEPPER MUSEUM

Robert S. Lazenby, superintendent of bottling at the Artesian Manufacturing and Bottling Company, was vital to the early success of Dr Pepper.

A Runaway Success

Morrison and Alderton experimented with the blend, conducting taste tests and making slight adjustments in the formula. As Dr Pepper's popularity grew, they decided to mix up large quantities of the syrup in the store's back room for sale at other druggists' fountains. The demand for Dr Pepper spread rapidly.

The two pharmacists had a runaway success on their hands. According to McCullough, they could not keep up with demand for the product.

"The popularity of the new drink was such that soda fountain owners from the surround-

Early photograph of W.H. McCullough at the Artesian Manufacturing and Bottling Company at 5th and Jackson, across the street from the 1906 building that now houses the Dr Pepper Museum.

and was born on December 1, 1830 in Big Spring, Virginia. Charles Pepper descended from a fine old Virginia family, and his wife, the former Isabella McDowell Howe, included Lord Howe of Massachusetts in her family tree. The couple married May 18, 1858 in Pulaski County, Virginia.

Charles Pepper received his medical degree from the University of Virginia in 1884 and began practicing medicine in Bristol, Virginia. He soon moved to nearby Rural Retreat, where he became the town's first physician and druggist.

Charles and Isabella were active in church and civic affairs, and Dr. Pepper was known as an "easy touch" who often furnished free drugs and treatment for families unable to pay.

Isabella Howe Pepper died March 19, 1903, and Charles Taylor Pepper died May 23, 1903. Both were laid to rest in Rural Retreat. An anecdotal history of the family compiled by Florence Pepper Raya in 1973 notes that Congressman Claude Pepper was a member of the large and illustrious Pepper family.[12]

ing territory purchased the syrup that Mr. Morrison had already named Dr Pepper. The demand became of such proportions that Mr. Morrison rented a building on Bridge Street in Waco, Texas, for the manufacture of Dr Pepper, as there was not sufficient room in the drug store for the supplies and containers necessary to conduct the business. It was at this place on Bridge Street that Mr. R.S. Lazenby first became associated with this beverage. He had been living in Fort Worth, Texas and came to Waco and was employed by Mr. Morrison at a nominal salary."[13]

Mildred Walker, curator of collections at the Dr Pepper Museum in Waco, noted that the museum was never able to prove that the Bridge Street location existed.[14]

Robert Lazenby produced his famous Circle "A" Ginger Ale at the Artesian Manufacturing and Bottling Company. According to McCullough, the formula had been purchased "by agreement of Lazenby and this writer from a man named John Proctor, who claimed he had worked for Cantrell and Cocrane in their famous ginger ale plant in Dublin, Ireland."[15]

Circle "A" Ginger Ale is still produced in St. Louis, and small batches are manufactured in Waco for the Dr Pepper Museum.[16] Lazenby named the drink after the cattle brand used by his mother's family.[17] The bottles carried this label:

> "'Aged in the wood.' A mellowed, ripened, distilled essence of piquant fresh ginger, spicy and aromatic. Deliciously extra dry. None genuine without this signature, R.S. Lazenby."[18]

In 1898, Circle "A" won an exclusive contract with the U.S. government to supply the Army and Navy during the Spanish-American war.[19]

Lazenby was born in Johnson County, Texas, in 1866, and grew up in Waco. Fascinated with chemistry, he taught himself the basics by devising his own experiments. He was knowledgeable

Dr Pepper was originally produced without caffeine, a fact that Morrison and Lazenby used to promote their product, shown here at the Provident Fountain, around 1910.

in history, literature, physics, and the social and physical sciences. But Lazenby's thirst for knowledge led to misfortune when he was young. While other family members slept, Robert would sit by the fireplace, reading by the flickering light. The excessive strain on his eyes caused problems with his sight. His mother took him to an eye specialist who prescribed the wrong medicine and nearly blinded him. He was plagued with poor eyesight for the rest of his life and became totally blind four years before his death.[19]

Lazenby was also instrumental in establishing Southern Methodist University in Dallas. In 1911, he donated funds to build Dallas Hall, the school's first permanent structure and a landmark still in use today. He remained a generous patron of the university, and after his death, his daughter, Virginia O'Hara, established an undergraduate chemistry trust fund for the school in her father's memory. The trust still honors the top chemistry student at Southern Methodist University.

One of Lazenby's last projects was an experiment for the federal government, testing if certain vitamins in citrus fruits could be preserved through a canning process. One result of these experiments was another new drink, made from grapefruit juice. Lazenby claimed it was rich in Vitamin D and christened it "Liquid Sunshine," a name he and Wade Morrison had used to advertise Dr Pepper. Lazenby died at the age of 74.

The Inventor Walks Away

Morrison and Lazenby joined forces to produce and promote Dr Pepper. But the man credited with inventing the drink, Charles Alderton, went a different route. In 1894, he resigned from the Old Corner Drug Store to become chief chemist for Behrens Drug Company of Waco, a position he held for 19 years.

While working at Behrens, he suffered a near-fatal accident when muriatic acid was spilled on him. His life was saved when laboratory assistants dumped him into a vat of clear water, where his clothes fell off him in tatters. His

Circle "A" Ginger Ale enjoyed an exclusive contract to supply the U.S. Army and Navy during the Spanish-American War.

sight was permanently impaired, but his other injuries healed quickly and Alderton was soon back on the job.

In 1913 Alderton left Behrens and accepted a job at Eli Lilly & Company, where he worked in sales for six years. In 1919 he joined Red Arrow Laboratories, a branch of Waco Drugs, which later became Southwestern Drug Company, and was employed there as a chemist until his retirement in 1938 at the age of 79.

Alderton died in 1941, two years after his retirement from Southwestern Drug.

Among the earliest examples of Dr Pepper marketing, this lithograph dates from the early years of the 20th century.

CHAPTER III
THE DR PEPPER COMPANY

"Flavor? You name it if you can. Rare, exotic, fruit juices! Spicy aromatics! Mingled flavors, savors, tastes and tangs from Orient and Tropic and all the world. It's tart but not sour, sweet but not sticky, bitey but not sharp; so unique you'll never tire of the taste."

— 1927 newspaper advertisement

WADE MORRISON and Robert Lazenby eagerly plunged into the new business of producing and promoting Dr Pepper. A small building on Bridge Street was apparently the first location where Dr Pepper flavoring was produced. In 1890, the company moved to Austin Avenue, where it remained until 1892, when it moved to Fourth Street. In 1900, it moved to Fifth Avenue, moving to another location on the street in 1906 and remaining on Fifth Avenue until 1965.[1]

Circle "A" Ginger Ale and Dr Pepper were manufactured and distributed from the same location. Other drinks blended at the site included Wine Coca, Celery Champagne and Zu Zu Ginger Ale, in addition to a line of fruit drinks and root beer. In September 1892, the company added cordial wine, Blackberry Cordial, and bitters, an alcoholic drink expected to boost winter sales, to its list of wares. All were produced from formulas developed by Lazenby.

Lazenby also produced a purified mineral water product known as Aqua Lithia. This was remarkable, since the exact same water was available free to the citizens of Waco. At that time, the town received its water supply from 20 artesian wells roughly 1,800 feet deep, drawing from the same source as the expensive bottled stuff.

As Dr Pepper soared in popularity, Robert Lazenby and Wade Morrison formed a new company. On April 14, 1891, the two soft drink pioneers created The Artesian Manufacturing and Bottling Company, with 50 shares of stock available at $50 each. At the first stockholder meeting, Lazenby was made superintendent of works and Morrison was appointed president and chairman of the board. One of Morrison's first acts as president was to establish bylaws for the new company, including a statement that the formula for Dr Pepper was owned by the stockholders, and could not be revealed.[2]

According to Walker, Lazenby bequeathed the formulas to William H. McCullough "and told him to look after Ellis Booker as if he was his own family. Ellis Booker was the first black man to work for Lazenby, and was very special to him."[3]

The formula remains a secret to this day. Charles P. Grier, senior vice president of operations until April 1995, said even the company's beverage scientists don't know the formula. In fact, he was one of only two or three people with access to the formulas.

"They are handled on a need-to-know basis. People who are doing work on a specific formula will be given whatever information they need at the time based on what they are trying to accomplish. But the complete formulas are generally only in the hands of the people who are producing the products. In those cases, each person doesn't have access to all the formulas. There are just two or three people that have access."[4]

The Unique Taste of Dr Pepper

Even consumers who have enjoyed Dr Pepper for decades have a hard time describing the flavor. "It's one of those products that incorporates so many flavors that it's indescribable," said Jim Ball, senior vice president of corporate communications.

"I guess spicy is the best. There's a heavy aroma. ... It doesn't wear out the taste buds or the olfactory senses. I guess spicy or peppy best describes it. I think the peppy comes from the fact that it energizes your taste buds, more than a pepper flavor, because pepper connotes something harsh and biting. The cinnamon and the other flavors in concert create an exciting effect that doesn't wear out your tongue or your pallet. I guess 'spicy.'"[5]

"We say there are 23 different compounds that are presently in the Dr Pepper flavor," said Grier.[6] A 1927 advertisement capitalized on this uniqueness.

"Flavor? You name it if you can. Rare, exotic, fruit juices! Spicy aromatics! Mingled flavors, savors, tastes and tangs from Orient and Tropic and all the world. It's tart but not sour, sweet but not sticky, bitey but not sharp; so unique you'll never tire of the taste."[7]

Above: Dr Pepper was one of many drinks produced at the Artesia Bottling Company in Fort Worth, then delivered around the state in both bottle and syrup form.

Below: When the Young Men's Business League of Waco sponsored a "prosperity banquet" in April 1911, no local indoor facility was capable of holding the anticipated crowd. As a result, the event was held along 5th Street between Franklin and Austin avenues.

W.W. Clements, who perhaps has consumed more Dr Pepper than any other person alive, still couldn't describe the stuff. Even after drinking Dr Pepper for more than 60 years, the best he could do was describe what it was *not*.

"I've always maintained you can't tell anyone what Dr Pepper tastes like because it's so different. It's not an apple, it's not an orange, it's not a strawberry, it's not a root beer, it's not even a cola. It's a unique drink with a unique taste all its own."[8]

Clements said Dr Pepper is not like other soft drinks. "It's the uniqueness of the product that gives it a special, not only taste, but once a person becomes addicted to Dr Pepper it's like belonging to a cult," he said. "There's just a bond there between the product and the person."[9]

Competition

The soft drink industry was made possible in 1772, when English scientist Dr. Joseph Priestley pioneered the technique for artificially carbonating water. Early carbonated beverages were regarded mostly as medicine, but they gradually gained popularity as refreshing drinks. In 1833, the first soda fountain patent was granted.[10] Soon, drug stores around the nation featured marble-topped counters, where soda jerks would mix carbonated water with flavored syrups.

The 1850 census showed 64 plants making carbonated beverages. At that time, the average American was drinking only one and a half bottles of these beverages per year.[11] As new products were invented, the soft drink industry grew. In 1876, Charles E. Hires of Philadelphia began manufacturing root beer. Other brand names, including Vernor's ginger ale and Clicquot Club Ginger Ale and Moxie, soon followed.

The two colas that would dominate the soft drink market in the 20th century were invented after Dr Pepper. Dr. John S. Pemberton of Atlanta first produced and marketed Coca-Cola in 1886, and the Coca-Cola Company was incorporated in 1892. Coca-Cola is now the largest-selling trademarked beverage in the world.

In 1896, Caleb D. Bradham of New Bern, North Carolina, developed a soda called "Brad's Drink," changing the name to Pepsi Cola in 1901. The Pepsi Cola Company was officially formed in 1903, becoming the second-largest selling soft drink on the market.[12]

Dr Pepper has long been dominated by these giants. Charles Grier explained that marketing makes the difference between winners and losers in the highly competitive soft drink industry.

"Hardly a year goes by that someone doesn't approach us and say, 'Hey, I have a new cola formula here that is every bit as good as Coca-Cola, or maybe even better.' ... And I tell them, 'Great. Bring along that formula and a few bil-

The Artesia Bottling Company in Fort Worth, run by Robert Lazenby's brother, Henry.

lion dollars and we'll see what we can do to catch up to Coca-Cola.'" [13]

Getting Started

Wade Morrison resigned on April 11, 1896, and C.T. Young was elected president. After Morrison retired, he helped found the Waco Young Men's Business League, which soon boasted more than 2,000 members. No gathering hall in Waco was large enough for the banquet held on April 10, 1911, so festive tables lined the streets of downtown. Every guest found a complimentary bottle of Dr Pepper at his plate, making this event the first major sampling of Dr Pepper on record. The event was repeated in downtown Waco in 1985, the 100th anniversary of Dr Pepper. Morrison died July 23, 1924, at 72 years of age.

On March 16, 1901, Young resigned and Lazenby became president. He was the dominant figure of Dr Pepper for many years to come. By this time, bottlers in Iowa, Illinois, Louisiana, Tennessee, Missouri, Nebraska, Oklahoma, North and South Carolina were using Dr Pepper syrup. Texas was the stronghold, with more than 100 companies bottling Dr Pepper by 1911. Orders ranged in size from The Carson Carbonating Company of Jonesboro, Arkansas, which purchased 92 gallons in 1912, 1913 and 1914, to the Little Rock Bottling Company, which purchased 336 gallons in 1910 and 368 gallons in 1911.[14]

On September 25, 1902, The Southwestern Soda Fountain Company of Dallas, with George Baker as president, changed its name to The Dr Pepper Company. This was the first time a company was called Dr Pepper. At this point, two companies owned rights to the Dr Pepper formula. The newly named Dr Pepper Company had exclusive rights to manufacture the syrup for fountain use, and the Artesian Manufacturing and Bottling Company, run by Lazenby, owned exclusive rights to produce Dr Pepper for bottling purposes.[15]

Dr Pepper briefly entered another business on December 5, 1906, when the Dallas syrup-manufacturing company purchased the stock of The Freckleater Company for $20,000. This company, which just happened to be owned by Baker, president of Dr Pepper in Dallas, manufactured an ointment for removing freckles from the skin.

These crowns, popularly known as bottle caps, are actually illustrations designed for a poster to celebrate the company's 100th anniversary.

Chapter III: The Dr Pepper Company

Early Dr Pepper bottles were sealed with Hutchinson's Patent Spring Soda Bottle Stopper, a loop of steel with a rubber stopper kept in place by carbonation. In 1892, William Painter of Baltimore developed a crown that capped the bottle from the outside, solving at last the problem of leaking carbonation. Bottles were expensive, and in 1910, Lazenby produced a bottle with the words, "We pay for evidence convicting thieves for refilling our bottles."

Left to right: An early bottle sealed with Hutchinson's Patent Spring Soda Bottle Stopper; two Circle "A" Ginger Ale bottles with holders; the 1910 "Thief" bottle; a Dr Pepper bottle with a paper label; a bottle embossed with the words, "Dr Pepper, King of Beverages;" a paper label bottle from Rock Island, Illinois; and a "10, 2 and 4" bottle from after 1925.

This company didn't fit in with the Dr Pepper portfolio, and the stockholders voted a year later to return the stock to Baker for the same $20,000.[16]

To keep up with growing demand to bottle the drink, Lazenby established a bottling plant in St. Louis, Missouri. Bottling rights for Dr Pepper and Circle "A" Ginger Ale were granted to Advance Mineral Water Company on October 20, 1904. The Advance Mineral Water Company then contracted with the American Mineral Water Company of St. Louis to produce and sell Dr Pepper in St. Louis. In 1907, the two syrup manufacturing companies were consolidated, so that the Artesian Manufacturing and Bottling Company was selling syrup for both fountain and bottle use.

The Bottling System

The "bottling system," unique to the soft drink industry, originated in 1899, when the Coca-Cola Company elected to franchise the bottling rights to Coke.[17] Under the system, companies sell the soft drink flavors, in the form of syrups or concentrates, to bottlers who add sweetener and carbonated water. The bottler then has exclusive rights to sell the new drink in a designated territory.

Bottling companies were often small and family-owned. The bottlers know the local market well, and used their knowledge to distribute and promote the soda. Bottlers can sell several different brands. Most are still independent, though Coca-Cola and Pepsi have been steadily buying up bottlers throughout America and the world. In 1986, 220 of the bottlers used by Dr Pepper were owned by Coca-Cola, and 180 were owned by Pepsi Cola.[18]

Dr Pepper has long enjoyed an enviable reputation as a company that cares about bottlers and works closely with them to sell the product. Bottlers took their work very seriously. "In my franchise area," one said, "you get up at 6 a.m. and you get out there and sell, knowing full well that the manufacturers of competing brands are as eager to outpace you as you are to outpace them."[19]

A 1937 transcript from a meeting of Dr Pepper and bottlers discussed the role of the bottler.

"The only function or operation for which [The Dr Pepper Company] is not fully responsible is selling. It should be obvious to any bottler that the parent company cannot be held responsible for the selling job. This is his end of the bargain and the part of the work he agrees to perform and the part for which he is completely and thoroughly equipped. We are not equipped to do selling except in our company-owned plants."[20]

W.W. Clements, former president and CEO, said in a 1984 interview that bottlers are so impor-

Above: Interior of the Artesian Manufacturing and Bottling Company, in 1912. Workers filled jugs with Dr Pepper syrup, attached labels and crated the jugs for shipping.

Right: Employees washing and inspecting bottles in 1912.

Chapter III: The Dr Pepper Company

Above: The Artesian Manufacturing and Bottling Company was headquartered in this downtown Waco building from 1906 until 1923, when it became the Dr Pepper Company and moved to Dallas. The plant continued bottling operations until 1965, when a large facility was constructed. This building is now the home of the Dr Pepper Museum, which opened in 1991.

Left: This 1912 photograph shows employees filling bottles with Dr Pepper.

Beautiful Dr Pepper metal decorated plates and platters today are considered valuable collector's items. The lithographed metal tray first appeared in 1939, and the calendar is from 1915.

tant, he established a policy in 1967 requiring that Dr Pepper get the best bottler in each market.

"In 1967, when I was put in a position where I could influence policy, that policy was put into effect. We want the best bottlers in the market. And since that time we've followed that policy and in most cases we've been able to implement it. Our real growth has come from getting the best bottlers in the market."[21]

John R. Albers, chairman and CEO of Dr Pepper/Seven-Up until March 1995, did not believe the independent bottling system would survive much longer.

"The Federal Trade Commission allowed Coke and Pepsi to buy as many of their operations as they have. You have the commission that allowed Coke and Pepsi to buy their bottlers, and since they're so dominant they have got the critical mass in any market to reduce prices to the lowest level possible and still make a dollar. ... When they voted to allow Coke and Pepsi to go into vertical integration, they killed or damaged the independent system significantly. Therefore, I just don't feel that this system is going to be viable."[22]

Coke and Pepsi have been buying bottling plants that used to be independent, including ones that bottle Dr Pepper products. This created an interesting situation, said True Knowles, Dr Pepper president in 1995.

"I think there's probably some good news and some bad news. They clearly are the most efficient and most effective bottling operations around, so being part of that system is really good news. The fact is, both Coke and Pepsi have spent $300 to $350 million each buying Dr Pepper franchises. So they have a vested interest in making sure it's a productive investment."[23]

Knowles said he would rather do business with independent bottlers who care more about Dr Pepper than with bottlers who are most concerned with, and employed by, Coke or Pepsi.[24]

Early Advertising

Prior to 1900, advertising stressed the fact that Dr Pepper contained no caffeine or cocaine.

Though both substances were legal, some researchers considered them dangerous. One ad that appeared in 1903 claimed that the drink "exhilarates, drives dull care away, sharpens the wit and infuses new life."[25] A 1905 ad took a broader approach, touting the drink as "the best-tasting thing you ever swallowed." The same ad noted that Dr Pepper contains "No caffeine. No dope. No heart-depressing drug."[26]

Early advertising capitalized on the fact that Dr Pepper was formulated without caffeine. "Dr Pepper stands alone on the bridge defending your children against an army of caffeine doped beverages, as the great Horatius defended Rome," reads an undated early advertisement, illustrated with a drawing of a Roman soldier warding off the enemy.[27]

But in 1917, Lazenby had a change of heart when he learned that caffeine was a natural product.[28] Caffeine was added to Dr Pepper until 1939, when Dr Pepper executives took the caffeine out and added vitamin B-1, reasoning that the drink would be healthier and therefore more popular. But as W.W. Clements recalled, the plan backfired.

"The removal of caffeine from Dr Pepper was certainly a bad choice in terms of sales. It took years to recover. But in the long run, I think this choice tightened the bond of loyalty that was evolving between Dr Pepper and the consumer. It's part of what humanized the product.

"It [Vitamin B-1] caused the product to go bad and changed the taste of the product. Now, noth-

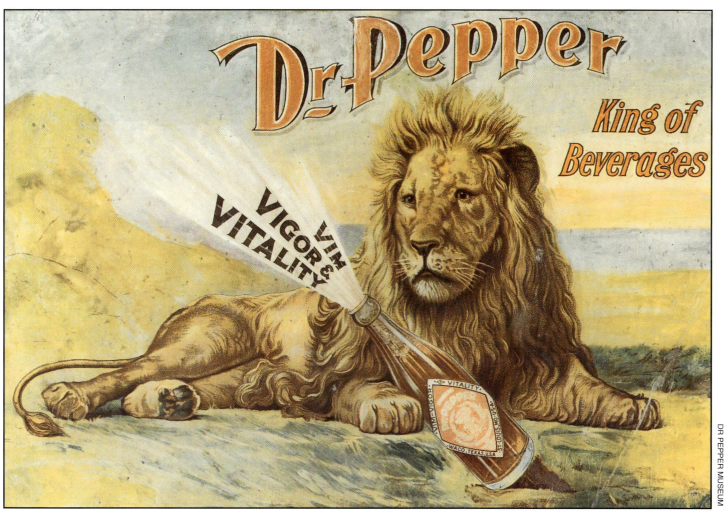

One of the best-known of Dr Pepper's early advertisements showed this majestic reclining lion, a symbol used for many years. This particular poster is believed to have been introduced around 1906.

ing was said about caffeine being taken out. The bottlers didn't know it. The people selling it didn't know it. ... It took several years to overcome the damage that was done."[29]

In 1983, the company introduced a no-caffeine version of Dr Pepper called Pepper Free in both a sugar-free and regular formulation. The move was in response to 7UP's 'Never Had it, Never Will' campaign, which pointed out that 7UP was caffeine-free. Though Dr Pepper officials did not believe that caffeine was harmful in any way, public perceptions about caffeine at the time prompted the new formulation. Most cola companies responded with a caffeine-free product. Seven-Up also created a caffeine-free cola, called Like, which it introduced in 1982. This product, formulated for the Seven-Up bottlers who did not have a major cola, was not successful.

From Dr Pepper's earliest days, it suffered an identity crisis. Some believed it was a health tonic, some a patent medicine or laxative and some considered it brain food. Dr Pepper was advertised first as one thing, then as another.

"Dr Pepper was sold as a health drink, a cure for everything, a restorative of vim, vigor and vitality," Clements said in a 1983 bottler meeting. "Well, that wasn't really a very good choice. In those days, just as in today's market, there aren't enough people who drink soft drinks for health reasons. ... Fortunately for us today, the product survived the 'magic potion' era. People simply liked the unique taste of Dr Pepper."[30]

Advertisements in the early years proposed many reasons to drink Dr Pepper. One of the more unusual was, "It leaves a pleasant farewell and a gracious call back," a line repeating on ads in the first decade of the 20th century.[31] "The public can rest assured that Dr Pepper is non-alcoholic, and that it contains nothing detrimental or injurious to the most delicate system," promises another ad published in 1903.[32] "Rare in flavor, with just enough 'tang' to make it delicious," boasted a 1912 ad.[33] "If Atlas were on Earth he would recommend Dr Pepper. Try it. It is liquid sunshine. It is what you want to promote strength," was the claim of 1913.[34]

The message of Dr Pepper advertising might have been broad, but the art work was magnificent. Posters featured pink-cheeked women, usually with flowing hair and lavish hats. These lithographs were designed as poster art, but many were also used on blotters, book marks, fans, post cards, calendars and metal art plates. Today they are considered valuable collector's items.

Among the outstanding poster artists was Philip Boileau, born in Quebec in 1864. While liv-

By 1918 the bottling operation had become much more sophisticated, with machines performing many functions previously done by hand.

DR PEPPER MUSEUM

In 1919 trucks such as this delivered the syrups necessary to create Circle "A" Ginger Ale, Circle "A" Soda Water and Dr Pepper to a rapidly expanding market, based primarily in the South and Southwest. Expansion in the North and East was much slower.

ing in New York in 1903, the 39-year-old artist met and married Emily Gilbert. Emily became his model and inspiration, and he suddenly found himself catapulted to fame. Boileau nicknamed his wife "Peggy," and devoted himself to portraits, prints and illustrations that became known as "Peggy Heads."[35]

Lazenby had always been interested in the English royal family, and he decided to use the king in Dr Pepper advertising. He produced a poster with a full-color print of an English monarch in all his royal finery. Embossed at the top of the print was the caption "Dr Pepper — King of Beverages ... at Fountains and in Bottles."[36] Lazenby continued the royalty theme in his next poster, which depicted a lion. The king of beasts became the King of Beverages, a long-running concept for Dr Pepper. The lion first appeared in 1900 as a 30-foot wall sign on the side of a downtown Waco building. Painted by Louis Sternkorb, the lion art was used extensively to advertise Dr Pepper until 1920. The lion was also used as decorative art on plates, print-ed promotional materials and throughout newspaper and magazine advertisements.[37]

The last official appearance of the lion was in 1993 as part of the design of the corporation's stock certificates. They were purchased by Cadbury Schweppes in March 1995 for $33 a share.

The World's Fair

The 1904 World's Fair and Exposition in St. Louis was a historic occasion, with 42 states and 53 nations taking part. Ice cream cones, hamburgers and ice tea were all introduced at the fair, and Dr Pepper enjoyed its first national exposure. Lazenby designed a watch fob with the fair's emblem on one side, and the words, "The Home of Dr Pepper, Waco, Texas," on the other. Attractive ceramic urns labeled "Dr Pepper's Phos-Ferrates" were given to Dr Pepper dealers as syrup containers.[38]

The Last Shoot-Out

In 1905, the Artesia Bottling Company was founded in Fort Worth, Texas. Lazenby's brother, Henry, who had been hired in 1902, became the Fort Worth manager.[39] Henry Lazenby was a good salesman, but he was too hot-headed to be an effective administrator. His frequent run-ins with employees led to his death.

On June 5, 1918, Henry Lazenby got in an argument with salesman Ed Ratliff. Words escalated to a scuffle, and Lazenby ran to his upstairs office, where he kept a gun. Ratliff went home and returned with a gun of his own. Ratliff walked into Lazenby's office, demanding $8.40 in salary. As he spoke, Lazenby pulled his revolver out of a desk drawer and fired at Ratliff, grazing his hand. Ratliff returned the fire, hitting Lazenby in the head. Lazenby remained in critical condition until his death on June 18.[40]

This lithograph, produced between 1906 and 1917, promoted Dr Pepper as a caffeine-free beverage. Caffeine was added to the formula in 1917.

Chapter IV
Ten, Two and Four

"Break Away for Three a Day — at Ten, Two and Four o'clock."

—Newspaper advertisement, 1927

WHEN WORLD WAR I ended in 1918, it became apparent that Lazenby and his company were in trouble. The company had spent heavily in Dallas and Waco on operations that were later moved or consolidated. The Dallas operation had been moved to Waco in 1907, and the American Mineral Water Company stopped bottling Dr Pepper April 1, 1920, when Lazenby purchased "all rights to the company in the copyright and trademark and license of the Circle "A" Brand and the words and name Dr Pepper."

In 1921, a deficit of $73,402 was recorded. On June 12, 1923, Lazenby and his group declared bankruptcy and the company was reorganized.

The new company was incorporated July 6, 1923, under the laws of the state of Colorado, most likely as Colorado laws were more lenient toward new companies. At the same meeting, the name of the company was officially changed from The Circle "A" Corporation to the Dr Pepper Company, and moved from Waco to Dallas, where it remains today. The Waco site, which has been on the National Register of Historic Places since 1983, is now home to the Dr Pepper Museum, which opened May 11, 1991.[1]

Among the men who helped Lazenby reorganize the company was Oswald Snider Carlton, a Houston insurance man who would later become president of a revitalized enterprise.

Robert Lazenby's son-in-law, John Bernard O'Hara, was hired to assume production and distribution responsibilities for the new company. O'Hara was an aggressive salesman who tirelessly promoted Dr Pepper. Woodrow Wilson "Foots" Clements, president of Dr Pepper from 1969 to 1980, credits O'Hara with bringing Dr Pepper back to life.

"He was very forward looking and had great ambitions for Dr Pepper. It was his vision and his leadership that finally got the company out of Waco and finally got it through the bankruptcy stages. ... They came [to Dallas] because they couldn't get the funding in Waco they needed. The banks down there were just not able to provide the loans and the support they needed, so they moved."[2]

O'Hara had studied to be a civil engineer, and he had held several engineering jobs. However, his career path changed when he married Lazenby's daughter, Virginia. O'Hara met her after he enlisted in the Pennsylvania National Guard and was sent to Camp McArthur, an Army training center near Waco. Their romance survived his three-year military service, and the couple married on June 12, 1919. Robert Lazenby welcomed his new son-in-law into the Dr Pepper business.

Together, Lazenby and O'Hara began marketing Dr Pepper in the Waco area. In 1920, they established a second plant in St. Louis, Missouri,

An interior view of the Old Corner Drug Store in 1917. At the soda fountain on the left, Charles Alderton first served the unique drink later known as Dr Pepper.

and O'Hara became its manager. In 1923, after the company was financially reorganized, O'Hara became vice president and manager, focusing on the direction and marketing of the company while Lazenby concentrated on production.

Carlton became Dr Pepper's first president on September 16, 1924. He had been a founder of the Great Southern Life Insurance Company, one of the leading insurance firms in the South. Though retired since 1921, Carlton helped Lazenby restructure and refinance the Dr Pepper Company. Carlton served as president until October 21, 1927. He died February 19, 1934, at age 64, at his hunting lodge in Livingston, Texas.[3]

J.W. Link became Dr Pepper's second president on October 21, 1927. Like Carlton, he was a Houston businessman, and it seems likely that Carlton kindled Link's interest in Dr Pepper. Link, who served as president until 1933, organized and expanded the business. With Link's guidance, plus a few investments, Dr Pepper expanded throughout the South.

Bottling Franchises

Link established some 20 Dr Pepper bottling plants during 1929 and 1930, with locations in San Antonio, Texas; Birmingham and Montgomery, Alabama; Memphis and Nashville, Tennessee; Charlotte, North Carolina; and Columbia, South Carolina.

When Dr Pepper entered Atlanta, Link called on his friend J.M. West, another prominent Houston businessman, to build a plant in that area. Members of the West family became major Dr Pepper stockholders. West was a member of the Dr Pepper board of directors from 1932 until 1937. His son, Wesley W. West, served on the board from 1941 through 1963.

Some of the bottling franchises established by Link are still being operated today by the families that established them. The Birmingham, Alabama, franchise is operated by James C. "Jimmy" Lee Jr., whose grandson will be the fifth generation to operate the plant.

Chapter IV: Ten, Two and Four

"Dr Pepper is great people," said Lee, chairman of the board of the Buffalo Rock Company.

"They have the best rapport of any franchise house in the country. They are just great people to work with. They have the best feeling among the bottlers of any franchise company in America that I know of and that's generally accepted."[4]

John Bernard O'Hara

O'Hara, who became president of Dr Pepper in 1933, was a man who was completely devoted to the product. He refused to drink it from a bottle, saying "aroma enhances taste enjoyment." He cited coffee as an example. "If you can smell the aroma of fresh coffee, your pleasure from drinking it will be doubled."[5] W.W. "Foots"

Circle "A" display in Waco's Cotton Palace, circa 1920. The Los Angeles and Boston notations indicate Circle "A" enjoyed national distribution at this time.

Clements, a Dr Pepper salesman at the time, remembered that O'Hara believed Dr Pepper should not be marketed like other drinks.

"He felt that Dr Pepper was a different drink from any of the others. It had its own characteristics. And of course he was right, but the other bottlers wanted to sell it like they sell the colas or they sold the flavors, and we still have to fight that battle with our bottlers today."[6]

"Mr. O'Hara was a man of lofty ideals," according to a Dr Pepper promotional booklet, from the late Forties. "In 1926, the company, under the leadership of J.B. O'Hara, began a program of public education and territorial expansion."[7] The expansion went so well that in September 1931, Dr Pepper opened a second syrup manufacturing operation at 2829 Second

Dr Pepper trucks loaded with bottles of soda outside the Waco facility in the early 1920s. The drivers were responsible for making sure Dr Pepper was properly stocked and advertised wherever it was delivered.

The Oldest Dr Pepper Bottling Plant

The oldest Dr Pepper franchise bottling plant still in operation anchors a busy street in Dublin, Texas. Bill Kloster, who operates the 104-year-old plant, insists on doing things the old-fashioned way. The plant, which opened in 1891, is one of the few in the world that still makes the drink with pure cane sugar.[8]

Before 1966, bottlers received sweetened syrup from Dr Pepper and added carbonated water. But that year, the company converted from syrup to concentrate, which meant it was up to each bottler to add sweetener. There were regional differences in the sweeteners, with some bottlers in the Midwest using beet sugar and some bottlers in California using imported sugar from Hawaii.[9] Most bottlers eventually switched from granular sugar to high-fructose corn syrup, which is cheaper. "As a practical matter," Grier said, "we can say that using extensive taste tests and statistical interpretations of those taste tests, that 99.9 percent of the consumers can't tell the difference. But I would

Sam Houston Prim, in the white hat was founder of the oldest Dr Pepper bottling plant in the world. Next to Prim is the father of golfer Ben Hogan, another famous native Texan.

Bill Kloster and his grandson, Mark, inspect bottles of Dr Pepper.

never say there aren't some consumers who in fact tell the difference.[10]

"Mr. Kloster in Dublin uses pure cane sugar and has a following of people who like the rush that they get from his original bottlers' formula for making Dr Pepper in 6½-ounce bottles," Grier said. "His clients say there is a difference and flock back to him."[11]

Dr Pepper Bottling Company of Dublin, with a valuable collection of rare memorabilia, signs and photographs, has become a tourist attraction featured in several national television shows and countless magazine articles. The decades-old machines fill 36 bottles a minute and operate only one day a week. On Tuesdays, between 400 and 500 people come through the plant to see Dr Pepper being bottled the old-fashioned way.[12]

"The bottle soaker was bought new in '47. We've been using the bottle filler since the Thirties. It's the only one of its kind still operating in the United States. We can't get parts for it, so we have to do a lot of welding and improvising." [13]

Kloster started working for Dr Pepper in 1933, when he was 14 years old. He worked for Sam Houston Prim, who founded the plant in 1891. "He didn't adopt me, but my father being dead, we became very close," Kloster said of Prim.[14] "A lot of people ask me the reason I'm maintaining the sugar in there, and I say that's the way Mr. Prim would have wanted it done."[15]

When Prim passed away in 1946, J.B. O'Hara wrote this letter:

Dear Mrs. Prim:

It is with deepest regret that I just learned that Mr. Prim passed away.

I have known Mr. Prim for a long number of years and always enjoyed a visit with him because of the sincerity, honesty and originality of his views on any subject that we happened to discuss. He was in my opinion indeed a gentleman of the highest principles.

According to our records Mr. Prim was the oldest living Dr Pepper bottler, and also enjoyed the distinction of having bottled Dr Pepper longer than any other one of our bottlers.

We all mourn his leaving us, and on behalf of the directors and officers of Dr Pepper Company, I wish to extend to you and all the members of your family our heartfelt sympathy in your great loss.[16]

Sincerely,

J.B. O'Hara

Prim's daughter, Grace Lyons, took over the plant and made Kloster manager. She ran the plant until her death in 1991, ironically on the morning of the plant's centennial celebration. Kloster and his late wife, Iona, took over that year.

Kloster said his old-fashioned methods are paying off. "Each year for the past three years we have had a nice growth over the previous year, better than a 10 percent increase," he said. And he plans to keep the franchise in his family, just as Prim did. "My grandson [Mark] came in the business about five years ago. He's my general manager and his wife, Diane, handles the office."[17]

Avenue in Birmingham, Alabama. The building is still standing and was restored as an office building in the late 1980s. The renovation was part of a civic restoration project to save prominent structures in the city.

O'Hara believed that Dr. Pepper should expand only in contiguous areas, a slow process that helps explain why Dr Pepper was available only in the South for so many years. But by 1935, the company could look with pride on recent accomplishments.

"Standing where Dr Pepper was 10 years ago, when it consisted entirely of two bottling plants in a small portion of Texas, and looking ahead to the development we have today in approximately 20 states, and noting the number of bottlers who are thriving on Dr Pepper alone, it should be clear to us that what we have done must be somewhere near correct. It is reasonable to assume we are traveling

J.B. O'Hara was president of Dr Pepper from 1933 to 1943. During his tenure, Dr Pepper expanded throughout the South. His belief that Dr Pepper was "liquid food" led to the company's great "10, 2 and 4" ad campaign.

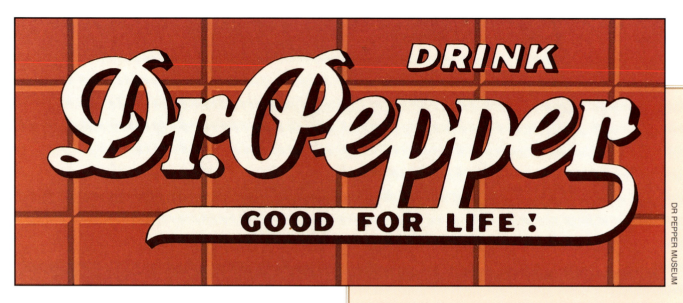

The "10, 2 and 4" advertising campaign was one of the most successful in Dr Pepper history. These 1927 advertisements urged workers to "drink a bite to eat" three times a day and return to the job with renewed energy.

In 1934, Dr. Pepper once again chose to change its logo, partly because the white script and red background bore too close a resemblance to the trademark of rival Coca-Cola. The new design came about by accident.

"The Samuel Stamping & Enameling Company in Georgia was interested in producing enamel metal signs for Dr Pepper ice coolers. ... They requested pounce patterns to assure accuracy in reproducing the signs.

"The pounce patterns furnished included lined squares behind the Dr Pepper logo which served as a scale for accuracy in the reproduction. Imagine the surprise when they arrived to find that the squares had been printed as a part of the sign.

"At first, company officials considered it amusing. Then someone commented, 'Well, you finally came up with something different.'"[19]

This tile effect was used in conjunction with the logo until 1950.

on the right track. ... Dr Pepper has actually been on the market for more than 45 years, but during the past 10, we have made considerably more progress than in the 35 preceding years."[18]

Clements remembered the cut-throat competition among the various soft drink distributors. One of his sales techniques was to convince retail outlets to put Dr Pepper on the right side of the cooler, where Coca-Cola was traditionally stored. The right side of the open-top coolers was more desirable because right-handed customers would lift the top with their left hand, reach into the cooler with the right hand and pull out the cold drink. The selection on the right was more likely to be seen and withdrawn. Another technique was to give Dr Pepper calendars and thermometers to the dealers, a constant reminder that Dr Pepper was available in those establishments.

Clements and other salesmen learned the "daily half dozen," formulated by Vice President and General Sales Manager W.V. "Smoke" Ballew. For every sales call, the salesmen were expected to offer a cheerful greeting, check cartons and stock, suggest a quantity for the dealer, put Dr Pepper in the cooler, check and place Dr Pepper advertising, and thank the dealer.[20]

Competition was fierce and often vicious, since Clements and his rivals worked on commission.[21]

"Pepsi Cola sent a distributor in there, and he had a big ring on his right hand with some lead attached to the underside, and he'd go back where my drinks were and hit them with that ring and it would chip the neck of the bottle which meant that when they opened it they wouldn't drink it. ... When I came in the next time, I had to take that bottle and put in another one for it, which was costing me money." [22]

The stock of The Dr Pepper Company was listed on the St. Louis Stock Exchange, St. Louis, Missouri, on April 16, 1930. This exchange, in combination with others, became the Midwest Stock Exchange of Chicago, on December 1, 1949, and

One promotional ad featured a dream come true for a young Dr Pepper lover who could have all the Dr Pepper he desired, served by a butler, no less.

Dr Pepper stock remained on this exchange until May 8, 1964.

Prohibition

From January 1920 to April 1933, the federal government forbade the manufacture, sale and transport of alcoholic beverages in the United States. President Herbert Hoover called it a "Noble Experiment," but everyone else considered it "Prohibition." Almost overnight, America became a nation of lawbreakers. Clements said bootleg distributors actually helped Dr Pepper sales.

"They were competitors, I guess, but they also were somewhat better dealers because people would come buy the whiskey — and you didn't have a mixed drink in those days; you would chase it with something. And I used to say, 'Well, you wouldn't chase it with Dr Pepper,' but they did." [23]

Old Doc

Until the mid-Twenties, Dr Pepper advertising campaigns and logos changed so frequently, it

Martha Mears and Dick Foran were among the personalities featured in "Dr Pepper's 10-2-4 Ranch," a radio musical broadcast in 1942 over 122 stations.

was impossible to measure results. Company officials eventually recognized the need for a cohesive campaign. In 1926, the company retained its first agency, Southwestern Advertising of Dallas, which changed its name to Tracy-Locke-Dawson, Inc., in 1927. Dr Pepper stayed with this firm until 1940, when it switched to Benton & Bowles. In 1954, Dr Pepper hired Grant Advertising, based in Dallas. In 1971, the company switched again to New York-based Young and Rubicam, the company that still produces its advertising in 1995.

Among the early image-setting steps taken by Tracy-Locke-Dawson was the introduction of "Old Doc," a fictitious country doctor who would appear consistently in Dr Pepper advertising. A few bottlers even used live Old Doc impersonators in their sales promotions. First and most impressive of these was W.L. Florence of Athens, Georgia. Florence bore a striking physical resemblance to the cartoon character, especially when decked out in black tails, pin-striped trousers with boot spats, a silk top hat and a monocle. Florence, who had a genuine flair for promotion, personally delivered the first case of Dr Pepper sold to a new account.

Because of early failures to give the beverage a specific identity, many continued to regard it as a patent medicine or health tonic. As Clements recalled, this turned away many prospective customers.

"Many people thought of it as a medicine and they didn't think about drinking it as a soft drink. They wanted to get to the point where you would drink it as a soft drink so they phased that out for that reason, is my understanding of it. And I know, for many, many years after that we still had a medicinal connotation which we had to overcome." [24]

Although medical symbolism was avoided in future advertising, Dr Pepper was not alone in making claims of health benefits to consumers, noted Clements.

Barns and other buildings had been the canvas for Dr Pepper advertisements since the early 1900s. In 1947, painter Bill Barrick created this pastoral scene of the familiar fading signs.

Below: Some bottlers used live Old Doc impersonators to capitalize on the advertising theme in the late Twenties.

Bottom: The Old Doc campaign was one of the first proposed by the Tracy-Locke-Dawson agency of Dallas. This centerpiece of a fountain festoon dates from about 1930.

"All the soft drinks as they came out started as being something for your good health. Coca-Cola was sold as a cure for headaches, and Dr Pepper was to cure everything that was wrong with you except maybe athlete's foot. But I think deliberately they did it, and then as the industry matured and as the people began to drink drinks for relaxation and enjoyment, in order to broaden the market they had to go to a different theme. I remember when I first started selling Dr Pepper, the message we received from Dallas was that 80 percent of the peo-ple didn't even drink soft drinks. ... Today I would guess that the number is close to 100 percent that drink soft drinks." [25]

Ten, Two and Four

Though the Old Doc theme was abandoned, Tracy-Locke-Dawson, Inc. deserves credit for creating the "10, 2 and 4" campaign that would remain with Dr Pepper for more than 50 years. In 1927, J.B. O'Hara asked Dr. Walter H. Eddy, professor of Physiological Chemistry at Columbia University in New York and an authority on nutrition and vitamins, to conduct a study on daily human fatigue. Eddy found that human energy dropped to its lowest point at 10:30 a.m., at 2:30 p.m. and again at 4:30 p.m. daily.

When O'Hara asked Tracy-Locke-Dawson, Inc., to find a way to capitalize on the findings, the advertising agency decided to hold a contest. Earle Racey, a copywriter at the agency, won the contest when he proposed the "10, 2 and 4" campaign. His prize was $75 and a letter from O'Hara.

The campaign survived numerous attempts at retirement, and is considered among the company's most effective concepts. Accompanied by clocks with hands pointing to the numbers 10, 2 and 4, the campaign championed the idea that drinking Dr Pepper three times a day would boost energy. "Three good times to enjoy life more," the ads claimed, over and over.

"Mr. O'Hara insisted that Dr Pepper was a food in liquid form and deserved professional and public respect. He aspired to achieve recognition of its value in its proper place in the daily diet. That, said he, called

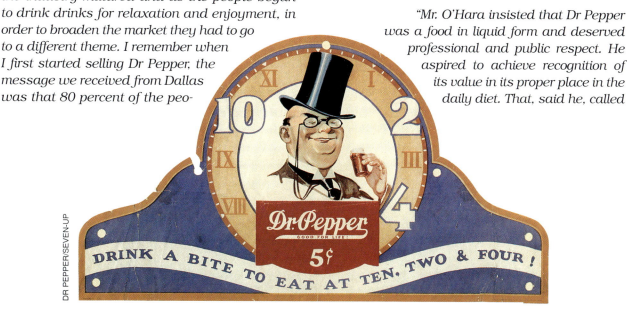

for one drink at mid-morning, and two more, well spaced, between lunch and dinner. Out of that was born the famous phrase, 'Drink a Bite to Eat at 10, 2 and 4 o'clock.'" [26]

Magazine advertisements in 1927 urged office workers to "spend five cents and five minutes on a bracing Dr Pepper." Another ad persuaded executives not to be angry when workers take Dr Pepper breaks. "Count it as a battle won. You'll see them return to their tasks with more 'fight.'" Dr Pepper, according to several ads, "actually releases predigested food into the system." And it's healthier than other drinks. "That bracing refreshment you feel is due to food value, not 'kick.'" [27]

"It was the most successful slogan the company ever had because of the alliteration of the 10, 2, and 4, and because of the appointed hours to drink. We made recall surveys of advertising on old slogans of all of the industry until maybe 10 years ago, and 'Drink a Bite to Eat' had a greater recall than even "The Pause that Refreshes.' Even though they spent millions of dollars more, it was just one that people remembered." [28]

The Liquid Bite

When World War II started, O'Hara found he needed to actually prove the idea that Dr Pepper was food in liquid form. Since sugar is a principle

J.B. O'Hara argued that Dr Pepper was essential to the war effort because it provided an important energy boost, as these advertisements from 1943 (left) and 1942 (below) show.

The "10, 2 and 4" campaign survived more than 50 years. Although the date of this poster is not known, the use of the tile logo places it between 1935 and 1950.

ingredient in explosives, the U.S. government limited its application to essential items, and soft drinks were not considered essential. Using Eddy's 15-year-old research, the Dr Pepper Company created a booklet titled, "The Liquid Bite," which discussed the importance of sugar as an energy booster.

"Early World War II experience taught us that fatigue was and is the great menace to maximum output of war materials. ... When food fuel is lacking, blood sugar is reduced, muscles and nerves fail to get their energy material and the human fires are banked down. ... That is why the person who drinks a carbonated beverage such as Dr Pepper actually returns to the job feeling refreshed. That is why such beverages have a real value in correcting fatigue and is especially true in emergencies such as war conditions." [29]

Largely because of this research, Dr Pepper and other carbonated beverages were declared "essential to the war effort" during World War II, since war production workers would be more effective after drinking a soda. The War Rationing Board established generous sugar quotas for soft drink producers, and O'Hara even convinced legislators to reclassify soft drinks as a food.

When the sugar restrictions were lifted in July 1947, it seemed that Dr Pepper sales would soar. Instead, the company actually suffered a decline in sales. Coca-Cola launched a great offensive, advertising in a big way, installing vending machines seemingly everywhere and establishing a world-wide distribution network. It was becoming clear that Dr Pepper would always be fighting the power and resources of the great colas, Coke and Pepsi.

This lithograph is one of many used by Dr Pepper for promotional signs and posters. The date and artist of this work are not known, but it appeared between 1906 and 1923, the years when the "King of Beverages" slogan was used. The emblem that looks like a swastika is actually a Native American symbol.

Chapter V

In a Class by Itself

"They wanted to put us in the cola category. Well, I knew it shouldn't be."

— W.W. "Foots" Clements

WHEN JOHN BERNARD O'Hara moved from the presidency to chairman of the board in 1943, an era came to an end. From that point forward, Dr Pepper was no longer a family-run business. Don C. Bryan became president of the Dr Pepper Company on September 1, 1943, after serving two years as executive vice president.

Bryan, a native of Oklahoma, joined the Tulsa firm of J.S. Bryan & Sons, wholesale distributors and bottlers, in 1917. By 1920 the business, which also distributed candy and tobacco, reached a volume of $1.25 million. Bryan was most interested in the bottling aspect of the business, and he was impressed with Dr Pepper. In 1931, Bryan left J.S. Bryan & Sons and joined his brother-in-law, A.L. Nims Jr., to open the Dr Pepper Bottling Company of Macon, Georgia. Bryan and Nims soon opened a second Dr Pepper Bottling Company in Montgomery, Alabama, and then a third in Albany, Georgia, and a fourth in Fitzgerald, Georgia.[1]

Dr Pepper's board of directors hired him as executive vice president in 1940. Bryan improved Dr Pepper distribution in retail outlets, and built better point-of-sale advertising for the product. "He wanted to be close to people," W.W. "Foots" Clements remembered. "And he wanted to be liked by everyone, and he wanted to be involved, and he was a great personal salesman. He worked all the time."[2]

Bryan was elected to the Dr Pepper Company board on November 20, 1940. He served as president during one of the most challenging periods of the company's history following World War II, when the industry rebounded from the decontrol of sugar in 1947.

The Dr Pepper Company was listed on the New York Stock Exchange February 14, 1946, beginning with 800,000 shares. By 1970, through stock splits and recapitalization, the number had increased to 9.6 million, and by 1972, 25 million shares were offered.

New Headquarters

In 1948, the company completed its magnificent new syrup plant and national headquarters building on Mockingbird Lane in Dallas. The lobby featured four murals depicting the history of soft drinks, painted by New York muralist Arthur Crisp, hired by Chairman J.B. O'Hara for the important task. "I think every detail of that lobby reflects the plans and vision and hopes and dreams that Mr. O'Hara had for this company," Clements reflected.[3]

The first panel depicted ancient Greeks and Romans drinking naturally bubbling water. The second panel depicted the technological innovations of bottling. The third showed consumers enjoying soft drinks from fountains and bottles. The fourth paid tribute to Dr. Joseph Priestley, the self-educated English scientist who determined how to artificially carbonate water and thus made the soft drink industry possible.

Born in England in 1733, Priestley became a dissenting, nonconformist minister. In 1770 he met Benjamin Franklin and took part in several of his electrical experiments. In 1772, he undertook the study of chemistry, and is credited with the discoveries of hydrochloric acid, nitrous oxide (laughing gas) and sulphur dioxide. In 1774, Priestley made his greatest discovery — oxygen.

He designated the colorless, odorless and tasteless gas "dephlogisticated air." Later, a colleague named Antoine Lavoister did the world an enormous favor by renaming the discovery "oxygen."[4]

Priestley published *Directions for Impregnating Water with Fixed Air* in 1772, and he was recognized as the first scientist to artificially produce carbonated water. But he became the target of attacks and death threats in 1782 after the publication of a less-than-respectful article, the "History of the Corruptions of Christianity." When a mob destroyed his church, home and laboratory, he fled to America and settled in Northumberland, Pennsylvania.[5] Crisp completed his paintings in 1948, the year Dr Pepper moved into its new multimillion dollar offices and bottling plant in Dallas. On August 5, 1985, as part of a divestment plan when Dr Pepper was purchased by Forstmann Little and Co., the Dallas headquarters property was sold to Harbord Enterprises, a Dallas real estate firm. When Dr Pepper merged with Seven-Up in 1986, the new company used Seven-Up's manufacturing facility in St. Louis. Dr Pepper/Seven-Up operated its headquarters from the Mockingbird Lane site for nearly two years until moving to its new location on Walnut Hill Lane in July, 1988. The murals also made the move.

Above: This mural of Dr. Joseph Priestley is among four painted in the lobby of the Mockingbird Lane facility the company occupied from 1948 to 1988. Priestley is considered the founder of the soft drink industry, because he was the first scientist to artificially produce carbonated water.

Above right: This panel shows the discovery of naturally carbonated water during the development of the Roman Empire, about 100 B.C.

Leonard Green

Leonard M. Green became Dr Pepper's fifth president on March 28, 1950. Green had earned a degree in business administration from Baylor University in Waco, helping finance his education by working as a student manager of the school football team. This is where he met his future wife, Doris Tatum of Beaumont. Unfortunately, she was dating one of his friends, the football team's star halfback. Green proposed a competition with his friend, saying, "If I outkick you, I get to date Doris Tatum." Green won the football kicking duel, and eventually the hand of Ms. Tatum, whom he wed March 2, 1931.[6]

Left: Leonard Green was president from 1950 to 1958. In the years following World War II, Dr Pepper began a national advertising campaign and saw a surge in popularity.

Right: Don C. Bryan was president of the Dr Pepper Company from 1943 to 1949.

When Green graduated in 1930, he was hired by Texaco and moved steadily through the ranks, becoming division manager in 1937 and assistant general manager of the company's sales department for the Midwest in 1947.

The same year, Green switched to Dr Pepper, where he was hired as vice president in charge of company-owned bottling plants. On May 4, 1949, less than two years after he was hired, he was elected executive vice president and a director.

Under Green's direction, Dr Pepper enjoyed remarkable sales increases, and gained new prominence in the soft drink industry. In 1950, when overall industry sales fell more than 1 percent, sales of Dr Pepper increased nearly 7 percent. The following year, Dr Pepper sales were up an incredible 23 percent.

The Fifties heralded a whole new direction for Dr Pepper advertising. A new position was adopted, that Dr Pepper is a unique drink, unlike any other on the market. "In the Fifties we finally figured out how to sell Dr Pepper," said Clements. "The Dr Pepper Company had always sold it like it was a Coke or a Pepsi, and it was not."[7] Dr Pepper began limited national campaigns. Television was just becoming popular, but the soda was not available in enough places to justify the expense of the new medium. Magazine ads were the main form of national advertising. Local radio spots were also popular because they reached a young audience.[8] The slogan in the Fifties was "The Friendly Pepper-Upper." In the early Sixties, the drink first became associated with Dick Clark's "American Bandstand."

Until Green's initiative, advertising and promotion was the responsibility of individual bottling plants. Dr Pepper paid for full-page advertisements in local newspapers, and developed a promotional calendar in 1950. The calendar featured four young women representing different regions of the country. Dolly Ann McVey, a native of Fort Worth, Texas, was chosen to represent the West. McVey, the widow of General Motors presi-

Above: Dolly Ann McVey, of Fort Worth, was one of four models chosen to represent regions of the country in this 1950 calendar.

Right: John Wayne is shown here on the set of movie "Jet Pilot," made in 1950 but not released until 1957. Wayne plays an American pilot who falls in love with Janet Leigh in this Howard Hughes film. With Wayne is Joe Golsch of Ohio, who won a part in the film as first prize of a nationwide Dr Pepper consumer sweepstakes.

other three winners were flown to Beverly Hills for the photographs. Cole is an actress and philanthropist, as well as chairman of the Dollie Cole Corporation, a venture capital and industrial consulting firm. She said Dr Pepper is "in my cabinet always," and added that she would have liked "free Dr Pepper for life" as payment for modeling.[10]

Another major change that took place in the Fifties was that the period after "Dr" was removed from the logo. Clements explained that the period was dropped while the company thought up a new logo to replace the tile design it had used since 1934. A slanted block-style letter was used, with the *r* represented as a line with a dot on the top right. *Dr.* looked more like *Di* followed by a colon.

"We came up with a block-type letter and the period just made it look like an i instead of an r. We were trying to figure out what do with that, and through that effort it was removed and there was a big discussion as to whether it could be moved or should be moved. There was a strong feeling on the part of some of us that it should be removed to take it out of the perception of medi-

dent Edward N. Cole, is now known as Dollie Cole. Contacted recently on her ranch in Texas, she said Dr Pepper held a national contest to choose the models, and photographs were submitted from all over the country. "I didn't even know mine had been sent in," she said, adding that a local photographer had entered her picture in the contest.[9]

Cole welcomed the chance to be on the calendar and billboard. She and the cine, of the doctor connotation. So, finally, after many hours of discussion and research came the question, 'Well, why not take it out?'... We took it out basically for the two reasons. One, cosmetic, to make the new trademark look like Dr Pepper, and the other, to get us away from the medicinal connotation."[11]

While Green was president, Dr Pepper introduced two vending machines into the market — a bottle vendor, and a revolutionary new cup vendor. The vending machines were challenging because they had to keep the soda cold and they had to keep it from foaming too much. Before an anti-foaming agent was added, the fall within the interior of the vending machine would agitate the bottle so much that when it opened, about half of the drink sprayed out.[12] The new vending machines boosted sales tremendously, Clements remembered.

"We learned that if we put one of those beside a Coca-Cola machine, where there had been nothing but Coca-Cola in there, that we would frequently outsell Coca-Cola because for the first time the consumers had a choice. And for the first time they got Dr Pepper served properly. That was a very important event in Dr Pepper's growth."[13]

Green expanded take-home sales of Dr Pepper with newly designed cartons for six, 12 or 24 bottles. Dr Pepper was also the first soft drink company to use cans.[14] Previously, cartons were designed to hold only six bottles. "Mr. Green was a very aggressive, far-sighted individual," Clements recalled. "He probably was a little ahead of his time in that he was more aggressive than the O'Hara influence, which was still very strong here. [O'Hara] was still chairman of the board."[15]

Green's aggression manifested itself in the way he measured bottler performance, Clements continued. Green canceled contracts with bottlers that did not meet his standards — more than 40 out of 380 bottlers. "Our contract gave us a perfect right to do it," Clements said. "But it damaged our credibility with the industry, with our bottlers first, with the competitive bottlers and with the suppliers. Where we'd been sort of the fair-haired boys of the early Fifties, we became the black-hat guys in the middle Fifties."[16]

Wesby Parker was president of Dr Pepper from 1958 to 1967. Under his leadership, Dr Pepper introduced new products, including chewing gum, lip gloss and Diet Dr Pepper.

Wesby R. Parker

On March 25, 1958, Green resigned to devote more time to private investments, including Dr Pepper bottling operations in Roanoke and Staunton, Virginia,

Happy Holiday Idea:

Hot Dr Pepper

THE festive way for customers to brighten up the holidays... the unique way to sell Dr Pepper during colder months. Heavily supported by national advertising and fully promoted by bottlers everywhere, Hot Dr Pepper is truly a Happy Holiday Idea!

Dr Pepper is the only major soft drink that was marketed as a hot beverage. To achieve the perfect flavor, the drink must be heated carefully to avoid scorching, and it must be served with a lemon slice, not lemon juice.

---

along with Raleigh, North Carolina. He was replaced by Wesby R. Parker, whose aggressive leadership gave Dr Pepper a new stature.

Parker had been executive vice president of General Foods, and he brought valuable food marketing experience to Dr Pepper. Hired as executive vice president of the Dr Pepper Company on July 1, 1956, his understanding of the subtle complexities of the industry grew by visiting bottlers and retail outlets, and by talking to the people who actually placed Dr Pepper on the market and sold it.

Parker began a management development program for key executives and managers in the organization, and expanded the program to include bottlers. Though he was involved in the total operation of the business, he focused his attention on marketing. He expanded national distribution of Dr Pepper and introduced it to Canada. "When Mr. Parker came on the scene, he was coming from a national company," recalled Clements. "Of course, his burning ambition was to get national, so his mandate to us was to go out, franchise every market."[17]

Among Parker's innovations was his 1958 idea of serving Dr Pepper *hot*. The idea did not fare well initially, but it later became a key part of the company's marketing program. Dr Pepper is the only soft drink that has experienced any degree of success as a hot beverage. The idea occurred to Parker while calling on a bottler during a blizzard. The bottler mentioned that a hot drink would be welcome, and Parker wondered how his favorite drink, Dr Pepper, would taste if was heated.

In his experiments, Parker found that the drink must be carefully heated to 180 degrees, without scalding, which would damage the flavor. The heated drink must then be flavored with a lemon slice, not lemon juice, to achieve the optimum taste.[18]

The problem with preparing hot Dr Pepper was that it was difficult to maintain this optimum temperature long enough to serve in large quantities. This was solved in 1968, with the invention of a heating unit which contained heating coils through which cold Dr Pepper would flow.[19]

As Dr Pepper in 1995 is sweetened with corn syrup, it doesn't taste the same when heated, said Bill Kloster of Dublin, Texas, one of a handful of Dr Pepper bottler still using cane sugar. "They don't advertise Hot Dr Pepper anymore because it's not the drink you ordinarily desire," he said. The Dr Pepper at the Dublin plant is the exception, he said. "We heat it and it really tastes good."[20]

Parker also installed a test kitchen and consumer service department, which devised several hundred meal and dessert recipes using Dr Pepper.

Parker, along with Clements, saved Dr Pepper from being labeled a cola by the Food and Drug Administration, a classification that would have hurt the drink's chance to distinguish itself, Clements said. Clements knew Lyndon Johnson, who was vice president at the time, and also counted Texas Governor John Connally Jr. among his friends.[21]

In the Mockingbird facility, 29,000 pounds of sugar went into each batch of syrup through one of these stainless steel units.

"They wanted to put us in the cola category. Well, I knew it shouldn't be. ... I called Lyndon Johnson's chief of staff and told him what my problem was. He said, 'You know Congressman Albert Thomas from Houston?'... He was chairman of the Ways and Means Committee in the Budget Committee. ... I had a meeting with Congressman Thomas, and he said, 'Mr. Clements, your president and your chairman already agreed to this labeling. Why are you here?' And I said, 'The board asked me to come up and talk to you. The reason the chairman and the president agreed to it, they don't know what the problem is.' ... It was approved and went into the records as a pepper-type drink."[22]

Creating a new classification of soft drink known as the pepper category was a major victory for the company, Clements said. "It opened the door to the ability to get the best bottler in the market because in most instances it was either Coke or Pepsi."[23] Unable to produce other cola drinks, these bottlers had no problem accepting a pepper drink.

How's it Made?

Dr Pepper concentrate is made in batches that can be as large as 3,000 gallons. One gallon of concentrate will make 154 12-ounce equivalent cases of Dr Pepper.[24] About half of the Dr Pepper concentrate is caramel color. Since Seven-Up doesn't require coloring, a gallon of extract will make twice as much soda, or about 416 cases of Seven-Up, Grier said.[25] James H. Wade, vice president of manufacturing, said it takes only an hour or two to make 1,000 gallons of Dr Pepper concentrate.[26]

The concentrates by themselves are so potent they are toxic, Grier said.[27] In fact, the concentrates could explode, though this has never happened. The process tanks are stored under ground, and rigged so that if they did blow up, they would "go up straight in the air," Grier said.[28]

Creating emulsions is the most time-consuming part of the process, Wade said.[29]

"We have to put an oil base together, dissolve some ester gum in that, then gum arabic in that, then go through homogenizers which beat the particles down to a very small size so the oil and the water and gum base will stay together, because oils are not soluble in water. So, we make this emulsion out of it and that stays in suspension in the beverage without falling apart. This may take four or five passes through these homogenizers and that could take a couple of hours for a batch to go through.

"Colas and lemon-limes are pretty easy. Root beers. Fruit punches, oranges, things where you see a cloudy product in the bottle are more difficult. Clear products are just alcoholic extracts of essential oils and are a lot easier to do."[30]

Of course, the process in 1995 is completely computerized, added Wade.

"We have a computerized control that shows us all the process tanks, all the valves, all the lines and pumps. They can dial in a formula from a number. It will automatically sequence through that, add the sugar, add the water, add the caramel colors, add the flavors in the order we have specified. It opens the valves, shuts the valves, turns the pumps on, turns the pumps off. The operator just dials the formula, hits the buttons and waits. ... Dr Pepper, some root beers, and Cherry 7UP, things that really don't require the emulsification step, are done that way."[31]

Back when soft drinks were formulated by pharmacists, natural fruit extracts, spices and other natural ingredients were used. "In the old days, the pharmacists prepared many of their preparations from basic, raw materials," Grier said.[32] A pharmacist would have been the only individual who could have access to all the ingredients necessary to concoct a soft drink like Dr Pepper.

Hundreds of 55-gallon steel drums filled with Dr Pepper syrup are ready for shipment.

Today, those flavors have been reformulated so that ingredients are easier to procure and more uniform in flavor.[33] "I think generally there is a consensus that says the flavors have been improved," Grier said.[34]

John Bernard O'Hara had been opposed to preservatives, said Clements. "The fact that it was made in those days from pure natural fruits and spices and herbs created a problem, the stability of the product, the shelf life of the product."[35] After O'Hara died in 1962, the company cautiously moved forward with adding an anti-foaming agent and benzoate, a preservative, to the formula. "My thinking was we should do whatever was necessary to make the product stable and to standardize the taste," Clements said.[36]

By the late Sixties, Dr Pepper could no longer promote itself as an all-natural product. The company had grown to the point that it could no longer rely on traditional supplies and natural production of a certain top-secret berry juice, Grier said.

"It was necessary at that time to come up with a formulation that essentially made use of some synthetic flavor materials that would in fact duplicate what we were going to miss in that juice. At that point in time we changed our label to conform to regulations. We now declare there are natural and artificial flavors in Dr Pepper."[37]

New Products

In 1963, the Dr Pepper Company introduced POMMAC, an artificially sweetened soft drink which had sold in Europe for more than 40 years. Originating in Sweden, POMMAC was imported to the United States, where Dr Pepper enjoyed exclusive distribution rights. Dr Pepper promoted and sold the drink for six years, experiencing only modest success. As it tasted sort of somewhat like champagne, it was advertised as the "sophisticated soft drink from the Continent."[38] The drink had a little cognac, but not enough to be illegal, Clements said.[39] But it took considerable time to recruit a POMMAC drinker, and repeat sales

Sugar sacks in the Mockingbird facility, late Forties. In 1995, the Dr Pepper Bottling Plant in Dublin was one of fewer than a dozen Dr Pepper bottlers still using pure cane sugar. Most bottlers had switched to high-fructose corn syrup by the mid-Eighties.

were slow. After six years, Dr Pepper discontinued distribution.[40]

"If they had positioned it as an occasional soft drink with a different taste and with a light taste, a lot of people would have liked POMMAC. But it was not a mass volume product."[41]

In 1965, Dr Pepper purchased Hustle, a high-energy chocolate-flavored drink, from Kapson Laboratories in Oregon. Around the same time, the company introduced Dr Pepper-flavored ice cream topping, taking advantage of the drink's success in milk shakes.[42] "That didn't go through our bottlers," Clements said. "That went through the grocery trade, and that created conflicts we didn't need. We had all these things when I finally took over the company. One of the first things I did at the time is, I took us out of those things."[43]

Other products sold by Dr Pepper at the time included Dr Pepper-flavored Lip Smacker lip gloss and Dr Pepper candy.

Diet Dr Pepper

Another product, introduced around the same time as POMMAC and Hustle, turned out to be more important to the success of Dr Pepper. Diet Dr Pepper remains a shining star in the line of Dr Pepper products, said Charles Grier, vice president of operations.

"If there was anything that put Dr Pepper back on the road to growth and significant achievement, it was probably Diet Dr Pepper. ... Bottlers who had been struggling to maintain the same amount of business they did last year, or get a 2 percent increase or 3 percent increase, suddenly were getting 10 or 15 percent increases. The compa-

Marketed as the "sophisticated soft drink from the Continent," POMMAC, which tasted a little like champagne, was not successful in the United States.

DR PEPPER/SEVEN-UP

ny developed at that point a reputation for innovation and being able to achieve something."[44]

When introduced in 1963 as Dietetic Dr Pepper, sales were slow. 'Dietetic' had a negative connotation with some people, who thought it must be a drink for diabetics who must restrict sugar intake.[45] "We were violently opposed to that, but Mr. Parker, who was chairman and CEO, thought that would send a more complete message to the public," Clements said.[46] After about three years, the name was changed to "Diet Dr Pepper." "Today, the diet beverages account for somewhere around 30 percent of the total market," Grier revealed.[47] "Prior to 1950, I would say it didn't amount to one 300th of 1 percent of the total market."

Dave Thomas, founder of Wendy's the well-known and highly respected restaurant chain, predicts continued growth in the diet segment of the soft drink industry. "I think the soft drink industry will change in the direction of diet drinks and better tasting diet drinks," he said. I don't think that diet drinks in the industry as a whole are the best tasting. ... I'm sure they're working on how to improve flavor and taste, as well as keeping the calories down. I would think that Diet Dr Pepper with the taste that they have achieved could be the leader in that category."[48]

Dr Pepper was among the first soft drink companies to introduce a diet product. Royal Crown Cola was first with Diet Rite in the early Sixties. "It was on the market before Coca-Cola's first attempt, which was TAB, and Pepsi Cola which was their Patio Diet Cola, and well ahead of 7UP, one of the last major entries in the field of low calorie beverages," Grier said.[49]

When Diet Dr Pepper was first introduced, it was sweetened with a combination of saccharine and cyclamate. In 1969, the U.S. government banned cyclamates. A second blow was dealt to diet drinks in 1977, when Canadian laboratory tests revealed that large quantities of saccharin, directly injected into the bladder of test rats, could cause bladder tumors in rats. The Food and Drug Administration proposed a saccharin ban. Dr Pepper joined with other soft drink companies to protest the validity and scientific protocol of the tests, arguing that a consumer would have to drink 800 12-ounce diet sodas a day to ingest the amount of saccharin given to the rats. The FDA put the ban on hold.[50] In use for more than 100 years, saccharin has never been determined to be the cause of bladder cancer in humans.

"Originally, our reformulated diet drink was a saccharin, cyclamate combination. Cyclamate was banned in 1969. So in 1969 everybody first of all went back to half saccharin and half sugar for the sweetener. That lasted for almost two years. ... Everyone pretty well reformulated to use 100 percent saccharin. ... When aspartame was approved, it was then used in combination with saccharin originally because the aspartame was so expensive. Of course in the meantime they began questioning the safety of saccharin, but it was never banned. Then our competitors moved to 100 percent aspartame. We did not. ... It was the introduction of a new Diet Coke that went with 100 percent aspartame. We retained the aspartame, saccharin combination two or three years and then moved to 100 percent aspartame."[51]

Hascal S. Billingsley

In 1964, tragedy struck the Dr Pepper Company. On November 3, an airplane crash took the lives of Ernest Marmon, executive vice president, Max McNeil, western area sales manager, and Max Green, national fountain sales manager.[52]

In 1966, Wesby Parker was replaced by Hascal S. Billingsley as president. Billingsley had joined Dr Pepper in 1931, working as controller. He became secretary of the company in 1940 and was elevated to vice president in 1947. In 1951 he was elected to the board of directors, became executive vice president and secretary in 1964, and on March 22, 1966, became president and chief operating officer.

Hascal S. Billingsley was president from 1966 to 1969.

Billingsley had majored in business at the University of Texas, and joined the auditing firm of Peat, Marwick, Mitchell & Co. in Dallas as an accountant. For three years, before he was hired by Dr Pepper, Billingsley worked on the Dr Pepper Company audit.

Between the time Billingsley was hired in 1931 and his retirement in 1974, Dr Pepper annual sales grew from $1.5 million to $138.25 million, and earnings increased from $387,329.46 to $11.9 million. Billingsley's lasting legacy would be the dramatic expansion of Dr Pepper's sales base. He was president for three years, from 1966 to 1969, then served as chairman and chief executive officer for one year. In 1970, he relinquished the CEO spot, remaining board chairman until 1974, when he retired. He retained a seat on the board until 1976.[53]

Collectors call this Dr Pepper promotional lithograph "The Sea Nymphs." It is undated, but the "King of Beverages" slogan places it between 1906 and 1923.

CHAPTER VI
GOING NATIONAL

"Well, I have so much feelings for the company and the product and for the people. I just hope they can sense what a product is, not just liquids and flavors, and signs and all of that. I still drink as much as a case a day. But to me it's just like that. It's a part of me."

— W.W. "Foots" Clements

WOODROW WILSON "Foots" Clements began selling Dr Pepper in 1935, retired as chairman and chief executive officer in August 1986, and continued as a director until 1995—a remarkable 60 years of association with the brand. On March 24, 1969, he was named president and chief operating officer and one year later he became chief executive officer as well. More than any other executive, he deserves credit for taking Dr Pepper from a regional favorite to a national brand.

"In 1970, I would say 60 percent of the business was in the five states down here," said Dr Pepper/Seven-Up Chairman John Albers, speaking from his office in Dallas before he stepped down in 1995. "We still do some 30 percent in Texas, Oklahoma, Louisiana, Arkansas, New Mexico area. But our growth has been significant throughout the whole United States. We've made some very, very significant strides."[1] True Knowles, president of Dr Pepper until March 1995, said, "Dr Pepper is 108 years old, but it's only been a national brand since 1970."[2]

When Clements became executive vice president in 1967, one of the first things he did was map out a bold strategy for the company.

"The substance of my report was that Dr Pepper was underdeveloped. It was underdeveloped because the prior leadership didn't really understand the product and they didn't have the perception of where Dr Pepper could go. ... I set forth a very bold, ambitious and aggressive objective."[3]

Clements' plan called for recruiting the best bottlers in the market to become Dr Pepper bottlers. He also asked for an additional $5 million for a special marketing program called the Dr Pepper Dominance program. "The beautiful part about it is, I never used a dime of that $5 million because we more than generated the additional profits by increased sales."[4] The company in the mid-Nineties spends $70 million annually on advertising, Knowles said.

Clements' history is closely tied to the history of the soft drink that he still consumes every day. Beginning in 1984, Clements was interviewed extensively by the Baylor University Institute for Oral History. The two volumes of transcripts from those interviews provide a fascinating look at the life of Clements, the growth of Dr Pepper, and the character of the Old South.

The youngest of nine children, Clements was born July 30, 1914 in Windham Springs, Alabama. His doting mother was so confident he would occupy the White House some day that she named him after the president in office at the time. "During the early years of my life, my father trained me to say, 'My name is Woodrow Wilson Clements, future president of the United States,'" he recalled.[5]

Since he was 9 years old, however, Clements has been known as Foots. He traced the nickname to third grade, when he wanted to play football. To qualify for the team he needed to pass three classes, but he had only passed physical

education and manual training. The football coach approached the school's spelling teacher, begging her to devise a simple test for Clements to pass so he could make the team. The teacher obliged. She spelled a word, and told Clements if he could name the word he could play football.

"The word she spelled for me was f-e-e-t. I didn't know what she'd spelled, and she spelled it again and I still didn't know, and the coach said, 'Well, come on! Get in there and try.' But he says to the teacher, 'How about giving him an example or something to make it easier for him?' And she said, 'Well, what is it that I have two of that a cow has four of?' The answer I gave her, I got the worst whipping I ever got in my life! So they decided if I didn't know how to spell feet, they'd nickname me Foots, and I've used that name ever since."[6]

In a *People* magazine article, Clements gave a different explanation for his nickname, saying he acquired it because his size $11\frac{1}{2}$ feet earned him the nickname "Slewfoot," which was later shortened to Foots. Regardless of how he got the nickname, Clements has long capitalized on it by sending Christmas cards in the shape of a bare foot.[7]

Clements' father was a U.S. marshal and justice of the peace. But he was also a member of the Ku Klux Klan.

"I'm sure my mother knew it because he kept his robe, which was the only way I ever knew it later. ... In those days, their belief was that they were formed for a good purpose. ... I remember when a black raped a white woman and lawyers came down from New York. The Ku Klux Klan got hold of this black, and of course hanged him, and I thought that was the most horrible thing I'd ever, ever seen. ... It got out of hand and my daddy got out of it when it did that."[8]

Clements attended the University of Alabama in 1934-35. While at Alabama, he and an enterprising partner started up a cafe. One of his customers refused to drink anything but Dr Pepper.

"I was buying drinks from all the companies. I'd buy a case from this one and a case from that one, and the man who sold Dr Pepper also sold Nu-Grape, Suncrest, Seven-Up, ginger ale, and some-

Above: W.W. "Foots" Clements began selling Dr Pepper in 1935 and retired as a company director in 1995. More than any other executive, he is responsible for taking the brand from a regional favorite to national fame.

Right: Clements with Bob Hope. Hope used to joke that Dr Pepper contained prune juice, and if a person drank it at 10, 2 and 4, it was easy to guess where they could be found at 11, 3 and 5.

times he wouldn't leave me any Dr Peppers. [My customer] would come in and she'd really be very unhappy. So I started insisting that he leave Dr Pepper. ... Then she would come in and if I wasn't busy I'd talk to her. And she started talking to me about what a great drink, what a different drink Dr Pepper was, and she got me to try my first Dr Pepper. And it was there that I acquired the taste for Dr Pepper and learned about the drink."[9]

Unfortunately, the cafe went out of business, and Clements was so broke he had to drop out of school. Some of his college friends purchased a bottling plant in Tuscaloosa, and they hired Clements to deliver and market Dr Pepper.

"I learned that if you could sell soft drinks, and particularly if you could sell Dr Pepper, you could sell anything. Because every living and breathing human being is a potential customer. It's not like selling Cadillacs where only a few people are customers, or not like selling men's shoes or anything of that nature."[10]

Clements worked for the Tuscaloosa bottling firm for more than six years, selling soda to convenience stores, restaurants and service stations. During this period, he married Eloise Davis of Tuscaloosa.

Clements had applied for a job with Dr Pepper on three separate occasions, and had been rejected each time. His luck finally changed in 1942. Every year, the Dr Pepper Company held a series of meetings for local salesmen and bottlers, known as the Traveling College of Knowledge. The meetings were conducted by the legendary W.V. "Smoke" Ballew, a man famous for his flamboyant style. When the college traveled to Birmingham in 1942, Clements was the speaker representing Tuscaloosa. Three weeks later, Clements was interviewed and hired. He reported to work January 24, 1942, as a zone manager. He worked with bot-

Above: W.V. "Smoke" Ballew was vice president and general sales manager in 1942, when W.W. Clements was hired by the Dr Pepper Company.

Left: The Daily Half Dozen gave route drivers precise instructions for every sales call.

tlers in North Carolina, Virginia, Pennsylvania and West Virginia, expanding and developing the Dr Pepper market.

Once he got his foot in the door, Clements moved steadily up the Dr Pepper ranks. In 1944 he became sales promotion manager, working in this capacity until October 1948, when he was named assistant manager of bottler services. In May 1949, he resigned from the Dr Pepper Company to become vice president and general manager of the Dr Pepper Bottling Company of Roanoke, Virginia. In September that same year, he returned to Dr Pepper as general sales manager. By February 1951, he was elected vice president and general sales manager and by June 1957, was promoted to vice president of marketing. Clements became executive vice president and a board member on January 26, 1967.

When Clements joined the board in 1967, he inaugurated a shift in Dr Pepper's marketing strategy toward consumers between the ages of 13 and 30.

"We knew that 13 to 30 didn't fit the demographics of all of the Nielsen's and everybody else. But we wanted to place a bull's eye around the young people and go after those people when they're first able to do whatever they wanted to. They could quit wearing long underwear, they could quit drinking milk, they could start drinking beer, they were out."[11]

He began selling Dr Pepper in school cafeterias, drive-in movies and drive-in restaurants. One of his many challenges was the general perception that soft drinks were not healthy. People believed carbonated water and sugar should not take the place of milk, Clements said. [12]

When Clements became president in 1969, he broke free of Dr Pepper's regional emphasis and promoted the drink on a national level. "When I became president, I said, 'Well, it's time now to get into New York City,' which for many people is the United States."[13]

A short-order cook named Dave Thomas was starting a restaurant, and Clements convinced him to sell Dr Pepper. Thomas credited Clements with forging the relationship between the restaurant, now the highly successful chain called Wendy's, and Dr Pepper.

"I think [Dr Pepper/Seven-Up] is more of a personalized, more of a family oriented company. I found that was particularly so when Foots was the CEO. We have always had good service or we wouldn't use them and their product.

"What made us get acquainted with each other was that you know he came from almost the same background as I did. You know, I was a grill short order cook and he was a truck driver. And he rose to the top of the company."[14]

In 1968, the company hired golfer Lee Trevino to promote the drink. Trevino would bet other golfers that he could beat them using a Dr Pepper bottle taped to the handle of a golf club. With the television cameras rolling, he would drink Dr Pepper (out of a Dr Pepper cup, of course) as he played the last few holes of a tournament.[15]

This trend was continued in later years, when golfers such as Chi Chi Rodriguez promoted Dr Pepper with similar

Chi Chi Rodriguez, one of several golfers who promoted Dr Pepper, sinks a putt into a Dr Pepper cup during a 1981 Dr Pepper golf outing in Indianapolis.

antics. The new national program required a bolder advertising agency, and in 1971, the Dr Pepper Company hired the national advertising company of Young and Rubicam.[16] "That was our first big step," said Albers. "We said we're going to put, no matter how thin a layer it was, a layer of national media on Dr Pepper."[17]

The new agency came up with the idea of describing Dr Pepper as "America's most misunderstood drink." Clements liked this approach because it appealed to young people, he said, explaining, "Youth always feels they're misunderstood."[18]

John Clarke, senior vice president for marketing in 1995, said Dr Pepper needed to establish a clear identity when it went national. The drink was hard to describe, so marketers were constantly in a position of telling people what Dr Pepper was not. It wasn't a cola, it wasn't a lemon-lime drink, and it wasn't a fruit such as orange or grape. "Dr Pepper was a really strange flavor. The 'most misunderstood' was your positioning. It was telling you what is was, by telling you what it wasn't."[19]

The agency also helped Dr Pepper come up with a new logo. "In those days there was much more to changing a logo than there is today," Clements said. "Today with everything being in a one-way package, it's not that big a problem because all you do is run down your inventories and then feed in your new one. But where you had returnable bottles coming and going, like this one, you see the new one and you see several others out there with a different logo."[20]

In 1973, Dr Pepper moved into Japan, even though Clements insisted he wasn't ready to tackle the new market because the company needed to focus on the United States. Before that time, Dr Pepper's only foreign business had been in Canada. But when Coca-Cola bottlers in New York began bottling Dr Pepper, international bottlers took notice. A man named George Otha, who worked for the Coca-Cola bottling Company of Tokyo, asked Clements if he was interested in franchising Dr Pepper from the Japanese Coke bottling plants. After much research and thought, Clements consented.[21]

With all the franchising and growth of Dr Pepper, it was only a matter of time before the competition would sit up and take notice. In 1973, Coca-Cola introduced Mr. Pibb, a product created to compete with Dr Pepper. "They came out with a vengeance because they wanted to say to their bottlers, 'You can't take on Dr Pepper because we have a pepper-type drink.' And remember, we had established that pepper-type classification," Clements said.[22]

In the early Eighties, Dr Pepper expanded by purchasing other soft drink companies. It purchased the soft drink division of Welch's Food Company in 1981, and worldwide Canada Dry business in 1982. IBC, a brand dating back to Prohibition, was acquired by Dr Pepper when it merged with Seven-Up.

In the early Seventies, advertising agency Young and Rubicam helped Dr Pepper refine its logo, creating the version that is still in use today. The agency also created the catchy and successful "Be a Pepper" campaign.

Dr Pepper had franchised only three Japanese bottlers, and all 14 of the others went with the new product, since they were Coca-Cola bottlers and Mr. Pibb was a Coca-Cola product.[23] In 1994, Mr. Pibb was still on the market, having sold an estimated 52.7 million cases to Dr Pepper's 617 million cases.[24]

In 1977, the company introduced a new slogan that helped define the drink to a national market. "Be a Pepper" proved to be a remarkably popular marketing device, noted Clarke.

"Be a Pepper was probably the greatest advertising campaign in our history because of its memorability and its likability. There was a guy dancing across the country singing this song that everyone remembered. That was really a campaign that was designed to recruit non-users of the brand to try it and drink it regularly. To be a Pepper."[25]

By 1966, Dr Pepper moved from sixth to fourth position among leading American soft drink brands and net sales grew from $28,660,482 that year, to $271,008,000 in 1978. "If you just follow the campaign lines of Dr Pepper from 1970, it pretty clearly shows you the development of the brand across the country," said Clarke.[26]

In 1969, Clements was selected by the Southwest Council of Sales & Marketing Executives, International, as the "Distinguished Sales & Marketing Executive of the Southwest." In 1970, he received the "Golden Plate Award" from the American Academy of Achievement, and was named "Marketing Man of the Decade" by the North Texas Chapter of the American Marketing Association. In 1972, he was again honored by the Sales and Marketing Executives of Dallas with their "Distinguished Salesman Award." In 1976, he was named Beverage Industry Executive of the Year.

Dr Pepper would be an entirely different company today if Clements had not survived a 1969 experience that nearly cost him his life. He had gone to New York on business, and while in the hotel his nose began to bleed. He saw several doctors, but they did not think the situation was serious. But when Clements was flying back to Dallas, he began bleeding again.

"That was Tuesday, November 11. They were not able to stop the bleeding. They gave me nine transfusions between then and Sunday night and packed the nose constantly. Finally I went into shock and they took me into the operating room on Monday morning and cut the carotid artery to take the pressure off. ... It was pure stress."[27]

In 1978, Clements separated from his wife of 40 years. He has since married his former executive assistant, Virginia Thomas. Clements, 81 in 1995, still loves Dr Pepper.

"Well, I have so much feelings for the company and the product and for the people. I

The ginger ale business was not new to Dr Pepper with the acquisition of Canada Dry. After all, Dr Pepper was first produced in the Artesian Manufacturing and Bottling Company, while also produced Circle "A" Ginger Ale.

just hope they can sense what a product is, not just liquids and flavors, and signs and all of that. I don't know, I still drink as much as a case a day. But to me it's just like that. It's a part of me."[28]

Charles Jarvie

In 1980, Clements was succeeded as president by Charles Jarvie, who, at 43, was a relative newcomer to the soft drink business. Jarvie had worked in sales and management positions at Procter & Gamble for 20 years. His miscalculation was his assumption that selling soft drinks was the same as selling soap products. Executives agree that he did not appreciate the unique distribution and marketing system of the soft drink company.

According to Clements, "He did not have the personality for this job. He couldn't adapt to the culture. It was quite a change from the Procter & Gamble mode of operation."[29] Jarvie "went and told the bottlers how to run their business," Albers said. "You don't tell independent businessmen. You work with them."[30] Dr Pepper relies on a network of franchised bottlers who are responsible for promoting and distributing the drink in their designated markets. The company places high priority on its bottler relations. "But Jarvie had an unbelievably large ego and he came in, and said, 'We're going to do this and this and this.'"[31]

Welch's and Canada Dry

Jarvie left his mark on the Dr Pepper Company by purchasing Welch's and Canada Dry soft drinks during his short tenure as president. "I think he wanted to have a billion-dollar business. That's the only reason he bought six more bottling plants," Albers said.[32]

In 1981, the Dr Pepper Company acquired the soft drink division of Welch Foods Company. Welch's was begun in 1869 by New Jersey dentist Dr. Thomas Bramwell Welch, who started the American fruit juice industry when he produced grape juice from 40 pounds of Concord grapes. His son, Charles, took over the business in 1872, and moved it from New Jersey to Watkins Glen, New York, in 1896, where Concord grapes are grown. The following year, he moved it to Westfield, New York, building a plant that processed 300 tons of grape the first year.[33]

Dr. Thomas Welch (left) and his son, Charles (right), founded the grape juice business that bears their name in 1869. Welch's Grape Soda is the No. 1 grape soda in the country.

Welch's Grape Juice steadily grew in popularity. During Prohibition, it was promoted as the only non-alcoholic fruit drink on the market. Besides grape juice, the company introduced tomato juice in 1927, and between 1962 and 1978, more than 36 new products were launched, including fruit preserves, fruit drinks and soft drinks.[34] In 1978, sales reached $170 million.[35] Welch's Grape Soda is the No. 1 grape soft drink in the country. Welch's sells jams, jellies and juices, said Mike McGrath, vice president and general manager of the division since 1988 and a corporate officer since 1990.[36] "We do about 60 percent of our business in grape," he said.[37]

Mike Galt, brand manager for Welch's, said that since 1988 the brand has introduced lemonade and fruit punch, as well as orange, pineapple and peach drinks. Tropical and black cherry flavors are scheduled for introduction in 1995. The brand has doubled in sales over the past seven years, he said, thanks to expansion to more than 85 percent of the United States.[38]

"Our battle cry is flavor leadership," Galt said, adding that Welch's is currently the top brand in grape, strawberry and fruit flavors.[39]

Dr Pepper formed a wholly-owned subsidiary called Premier Beverages when it acquired Welch's in 1981. Premier Beverages also began marketing IBC Root Beer brands in 1987, a brand it acquired with the Seven-Up merger in 1986. IBC, or the

Unbearably Good Dr Pepper

The mascot for Waco-based Baylor University finds his job more "bearable" when he is fortified with a cool Dr Pepper. Baylor, the largest Baptist university in the nation, enjoys a close relationship with the Dr Pepper Company, and generations of Baylor bears have had a sweet tooth for the locally produced soft drink.

The bears are cuddly cubs when they are acquired by Baylor, but they soon grow enormous. Handlers have found that bribing the animals with a bottle (or two or three) of Dr Pepper makes them easier to handle.

Above, Right: In the early Twenties, a Baylor bear enjoys the unique taste of Dr Pepper.

Above: Decades later, another mascot finds the drink just as enjoyable.

Independent Breweries Company of St. Louis, was developed in 1919 as an alternative to alcohol during Prohibition. Seven-Up had purchased IBC from Taylor Beverages in 1980. IBC in 1995 manufactures Cream Soda and Root Beer in diet and regular versions.

IBC uses its own bottlers, and Welch's is heading in the same direction, McGrath said. "You clearly have control of your own destiny. That's not a knock on the bottler system at all, it's just that if you don't have control you don't have ownership."[40] IBC sells directly to the stores, using brokers as surrogate sales help. "They go to the trade, they present our deals, our promotions, our pricing, our packaging. For that they receive a percentage of our sales."[41]

On February 2, 1982, Dr Pepper bought the Canada Dry Corporation from Norton Simon, Inc. for $155 million. Clements said it was a smart move for Dr Pepper.

"Canada Dry's strengths are where our weaknesses were, both geographically and in the marketplace. They're strong in the East and the North and internationally, and that's where we're weakest. They're strong in the bars, taverns, restaurants and hotels, and that's where we're weakest. I felt it could complement us. I thought it was a positive thing."[42]

However, Clements added, the timing was wrong, and Dr Pepper was forced to divert resources from the development of Dr Pepper in order to boost Canada Dry. Another challenge of the acquisition was that Canada Dry employees resented the purchase, since the company had once been bigger than Dr Pepper.

Jarvie's efforts increased volume among national accounts, but not enough to offset the sharp decline in bottler sales. The strategy resulted in a loss of Dr Pepper's overall market share. He was spending too much money, expanding the company too fast, according to Clements. "Our volume was going down and our costs were going up. ... He brought in people and paid them more money than the people they were working for, which created a morale problem."[43] The board asked for Jarvie's resignation in November 1982. He was replaced by Richard Q. Armstrong, who had been president of Canada Dry.

Richard Armstrong, former president of Canada Dry, was president of Dr Pepper from 1982 to 1984.

Richard Q. Armstrong

A native of Boston and an honors graduate of Bowdoin College in Brunswick, Maine, he had worked 13 years in senior account positions at major advertising agencies before becoming vice president and director of marketing for Dobbs-Life Savers International, a unit of Squibb. In 1976, Armstrong joined Canada Dry as president of its international division. Three years later he became president and chief operating officer. He was credited with a dramatic turnaround of Canada Dry's domestic operations.

Armstrong became president of Dr Pepper while remaining head of Canada Dry. He remained in the post until February 28, 1984, when stockholders approved a tender offer from Forstmann Little & Company for the purchase of all outstanding shares of stock of Dr Pepper.

The First Leveraged Buy Out

Dr Pepper entered into an agreement with the New York investment firm to accept $22 per share for the Dr Pepper Company, for a total of $647 million. W.W. "Foots" Clements had decided to sell the company. Though it was asset-rich, the company was growing slowly, and the board was concerned about the possibility of a hostile takeover by larger rival brands. "I told the board I thought it was time to sell," he said, "and they agreed."[44]

Dr Pepper went private February 29, 1984, and was removed from the New York Stock Exchange. The night before the final directors' dinner, a party was planned to commemorate the event. Thinking of the expression, "It ain't over until the fat lady sings," Clements hired Melody Jones, an overweight opera singer (who didn't mind being called fat) to entertain the guests. It was an emotional evening. She performed again the following morning at the final meeting of shareholders who openly wept at the "closing" of their company.

Twenty-five-year Dr Pepper veteran Jim Ball, vice president of corporate communications, explained that Forstmann Little executives Theodore J. Forstmann, Nicholas C. Forstmann and William Brian Little planned to increase the value of Dr Pepper and then sell it.

"These guys had just put together their operation with an eye on developing a leveraged buyout. ... They infused money and paid off debt by selling assets. People realized the whole dynamic of the company would change. And it did. We divested ourselves of the Canada Dry company, our corporate property and headquarters, and the 10 company-owned plants. ... The backers in turn received the benefit from the creation of stock. These people invested in the company and got a pretty quick payback on it. ... All the financial backers want to do is recoup their investment within a specified period of time. And that was from 1984 to 1986."[45]

Two months after Forstmann Little acquired Dr Pepper, it sold Canada Dry to RJR Nabisco. "Canada Dry was part of the deal and going right away," said John Albers, chairman and CEO. "When they came in, they said, 'We're going to sell everything except Dr Pepper,' and that's what they did."[46]

Joe Hughes was president and chief operating officer of Dr Pepper from March to December 1984. Hired in 1968, he was instrumental in streamlining the company after it went private in 1984.

Ira Rosenstein, the company's chief financial officer until May 1995, was instrumental in streamlining the company after it was purchased by Forstmann Little. Rosenstein had joined Dr Pepper in 1980, working with a bottling franchise in California. In 1984, he was promoted to chief financial officer and vice president of finance.

"In 1984 when we took the company private, we just had a basic concentrate facility, but we owned 10 bottling plants. ... When I came here, one of my missions was to sell off our bottling plants. I sold off my own company in Southern California to Coca-Cola enterprises. ... In 18 months, we sold 10 bottling plants and raised close to $450 million. ... In fact, one of the assets we sold was the Mockingbird facility."[48]

Ira Rosenstein proved a remarkably resourceful member of the management team, and was instrumental in streamlining the company.

"I was involved in the financial side there, and a little of the operation side. Then in 1984, when the company was going private, they asked me if I wanted to come down as the chief financial officer of the company. At the same time, John Albers was involved in the sales and marketing side of the business, and they made him president and chief operating officer. So we sort of became partners at that time and have continued to be partners for the last 11 years."[49]

"I think [divesting Canada Dry] made a lot of sense," said John Clarke, who had been director of marketing at Canada Dry and is now senior vice president for marketing at Dr Pepper. He moved to Dr Pepper 18 months before the company purchased Canada Dry. "As part of the ability to make the LBO work it required some divestitures."[47]

When the company sold Canada Dry, Richard Armstrong left. Joe Hughes was made president and chief operating officer of the Dr Pepper Company on March 6, 1984. "Joe was kind of a

Theodore J. Forstmann, Nicholas C. Forstmann and William Brian Little (left to right) were partners in the New York investment firm of Forstmann Little and Company, which purchased Dr Pepper in 1984. The partners streamlined the company and management and sold it to investors, including Thomas O. Hicks and Robert J. Haas.

CHAPTER VI: GOING NATIONAL 75

caretaker through the process of getting the corporate plants and Canada Dry sold," said Ball. "That was to be his role."[50]

A graduate of Southern Methodist University in Dallas, Hughes began his career working as an editor for the *Dallas Times Herald*. His affiliation with Dr Pepper, however, dates back to 1954 when, as manager of the Dallas office of Harshe Rotman, Inc., a Chicago public relations firm, he handled the Dr Pepper account. He joined Dr Pepper in 1968 as vice president of franchising. A year later, he became vice president of marketing services. He was promoted to vice president of marketing in 1970, and was elected executive vice

As part of Forstmann Little and Company's divestment plan, the Mockingbird Lane headquarters property was sold to Harbord Enterprises, a Dallas real estate firm. Dr Pepper was allowed to lease the facility for 10 years, but after it merged with Seven-Up, both companies moved to Walnut Hill Lane in July 1988. In these pictures, the famous "10, 2 and 4" clock, showing when to drink a Dr Pepper, is being removed from the Mockingbird facility after the company moved to its new address in 1988.

John R. Albers, president from 1983 to 1990, was chairman and CEO of the Dr Pepper/Seven-Up Companies Inc. until 1995, when it was acquired by Cadbury Schweppes.

president in 1973. On December 3, 1984, Hughes was elected vice chairman and John Albers was named president. As Ball remembered, Forstmann Little remained focused on the future.

"I don't think [Hughes] was ready to retire, but I think Forstmann had a real liking for John [Albers] and saw John as the future of the company. After the divestitures were made in corporate plants, headquarters, and Canada Dry, they saw John as the person who would take us to the next level, which he obviously did."[51]

John R. Albers

Albers, chairman and CEO until March 1995, said he had "a great deal of respect for [Forstmann Little's] financial acumen, but they did not have respect for the human aspect of it. I saw them fire some good people. ... How I survived I don't know, because I'm rather outspoken, but I also produce results, so maybe that's why I'm still here."[52]

"A theory that I have on operating a business is that you hire good people and let them take chances. We have an operating philosophy around the company that everybody is here for a purpose.

"From the standpoint of creativity we allow mistakes around here. But we also hire good and intelligent people. ... You can make as many mistakes as you want, just don't make the same one twice. If you make it twice you better have a pretty good argument why, because it has a real impact on your future around the company. Of course if you make the same mistake three times, it's death.

"If employees don't like us I'd just as soon have them go, because I see no future for them. I do believe that firing is a very, very positive strategy in a company and strategically it's good for the employee and the company. Because if you've got somebody that's not going to work, it's better for him to get out because he won't go anyplace, and it's better for you to get him out so he's not disruptive."[53]

Albers attended the University of Minnesota, concentrating on courses in business and economics before being recruited and serving two years in the U.S. Army as a first lieutenant. He eventually graduated from Minnesota and undertook postgraduate work at Stanford University in California. Albers began his business career in 1959 with Campbell-Mithun Advertising in Minn-eapolis, where he worked as an account executive on the Pillsbury account. In 1964 he joined Grant Advertising in Dallas as vice president and account executive for Dr Pepper and Burrus Mills. He returned to Minneapolis in 1965 as account supervisor for Knox-Reeves on the General Mills, Pillsbury and Alberto-Culver accounts. In 1969 Albers co-founded Zapata International, a franchise Mexican restaurant chain.

Albers joined the Dr Pepper Company on May 1, 1971, as vice president of advertising. In 1974 he was named vice president of marketing, and in September 1980 he became senior vice president of marketing. He left Dr Pepper in 1982 to manage a venture capital firm. According to *Forbes*, he left because he felt the company was spending too much money acquiring bottlers and not enough on advertising.[54] Albers later returned to the company in unusual circumstances, as he explained.

"I was out buying businesses and there was a wonderful little specialty business called Michael's. And I came to Foots and said, 'Foots, I need some additional cash. Would you put in some money?' ... And he said, 'John, I've got a problem. I've just gone through a divorce, my wife has taken some of my funds, and I can't afford to get involved with you on this, but let me tell you what's happening here. Jarvie is no longer with us, the gentleman who is today president of Dr Pepper USA is leaving us. If you don't raise the money, are you interested in coming back as president of Dr Pepper USA?' I said, 'Well, I'm going to raise the money, but I'll think about it.' I didn't raise the money and that's how I came back as president of Dr Pepper USA."[55]

Albers returned in May 1983 as president of Dr Pepper USA, responsible for providing sales and marketing support to some 450 licensed Dr Pepper bottlers in the United States In March 1984, Albers was made corporate executive vice president. "In less than two years, he cut overhead in half and put the $13 million annual savings into marketing Dr Pepper," according to a 1994 *Forbes* article.[56]

One streamlining measure was to sell the company's flagship bottling operations in Waco, Dallas and Fort Worth, Texas. These assets were sold to Dallas investors Hicks & Haas in March 1985, for $100 million. Thomas Hicks and Robert Haas would soon be instrumental in the company's merge with Seven-Up.

Around the same time, Dr Pepper tried a more aggressive marketing strategy, said John Clarke, vice president in charge of marketing.

"The repositioning was very simple. Instead of trying to compete with Coke and Pepsi for displays, we wanted to sell in cooperation with Coke and Pepsi. Sell on the same display. So, when they had to go to our same bottler who was the Coke bottler,

James A. Ball III, senior vice president for corporate communications, has been instrumental in shaping the image and character of the company for more than 25 years.

he had a Coke display that had some Dr Pepper on it. When the Pepsi bottler who was the Dr Pepper bottler had a display there would be some Dr Pepper on it. Instead of fighting them for display, we decided to spend our time and energy to try and participate in the overall display program."[57]

The scaled-down Dr Pepper attracted the attention of several companies, and in 1986, Dr Pepper was purchased by equity owners consisting of several banks, Dr Pepper corporate management and Hicks & Haas, a Dallas investment firm that had, that same year, purchased another great name in the soft drink industry — Seven-Up.

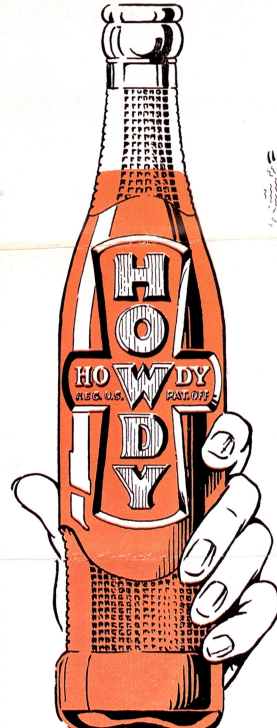

1929 Advertising Number

New Howdy Hi-Bottle
Stacks Perfectly

The Howdy bottle of 1927-1928 was all right with one exception. It would not stack or rack. The bottles toppled to the small end. So many bottlers complained of this one feature that we have changed it to secure long straight sides that insure good stacking.

The maltese cross is counter-sunk in the plain glass and the Howdy in acrostic is bossed high, making a glass label effect that registers on the eye and remains in the memory.

Manufacturers of bottles have complained of the height of the old bottle—9 inches—because it compelled a special run and several sets of molds. By taking off 3/8 of an inch, this may be run in with other molds and small runs can be supplied to bottlers without delay.

To be able to reorder during the season in small quantities and get them promptly seems to justify the change in height.

This new bottle is not obligatory. Any bottler may order the old style, or, if his quantity justifies, can have this new bottle made 9 inches.

Remember that a bottler may buy:

The '27-'28 bottle or—

The '29 bottle 8 5/8 inches high or—

The '29 bottle 9 inches high if he orders a quantity that justifies the run.

The Howdy Hi-bottle looks as big as any big bottle—holds 7 ounces filled to top or 6½ at 2 inches below. No bottle is more inviting—no bottle registers better. Complete Identity is the result—and it is Identity that brings top prices.

Keep this for reference—
You will want to know about Howdy
or Seven-Up before the season is over.

In 1920, nine years before Charles L. Grigg invented Seven-Up, he formulated the orange-flavored Howdy. This 1929 notice informed bottlers of a packaging innovation. Grigg had already established a strong network of bottlers by the time he introduced Seven-Up.

CHAPTER VII
THE FOUNDING OF SEVEN-UP

"Stick to the formula and fear no competition."

— Charles L. Grigg, founder of Seven-Up

THE FOUNDER of 7UP, Charles Leiper Grigg, was born in 1868 in a log cabin in Price's Branch, Missouri. The town had a total population of 25, not counting livestock, making it so small that most Missourians had never heard of it. When Grigg was 22, he started a modest general store, drawing customers from outlying rural regions. When he received catalogs from St. Louis wholesalers, he was disappointed in the quality of sales promotions and literature. He wrote to admonish one of the wholesalers, pointing out several ways the catalog could be improved. The company wrote him a terse reply: "If you think you can do better, come to St. Louis and do it." Never one to ignore a challenge, Grigg packed his bags and left Price's Branch for the big city.[1]

Grigg ventured into advertising, working for several local agencies, and was introduced to the carbonated beverage business. In 1918 and 1919, Grigg was the star salesman of a manufacturing firm headed by a man named Vess Jones. Grigg conceived, created and marketed an orange drink called Whistle. It quickly became the company's top seller, and Grigg became sales and marketing manager, the company's No. 2 post. Once promoted, however, Grigg's relationship with Jones became so badly strained that Grigg left behind his beloved orange drink and began looking for a new career.[2]

Grigg approached the Warner-Jenkinson Company of St. Louis, a successful enterprise founded in 1905 to develop flavoring agents for soft drinks, candy and ice cream. The only employee on the premises when he arrived was 23-year-old Garret F. Meyer, nephew of company President W.F. Meyer and future president of the company.

"There I was alone in the office," Meyer recalled years later, "when Grigg walks in and tells me he's looking for a company that can supply him with a high-quality concentrate for an orange-flavored soft drink. He wanted to establish a continuing relationship with an outfit that could function as his primary supplier."[3]

Meyer told Grigg that Warner-Jenkinson was the place. To make the drink, Warner-Jenkinson purchased a homogenizer, which emulsified essential citrus oils from the peels of the orange. In a matter of months, Grigg invented a new carbonated orange drink with a 14 percent sugar content and gave it the trademark of Howdy. Grigg appreciated the fact that trademarks must be simple, succinct, and original. He also believed a trademark should not, in any way, describe the product itself.

Grigg did not have enough capital to properly launch his new drink. While lunching at the City Club in St. Louis, he met Edmund G. Ridgway. Born in 1875, Ridgway had been a railroad telegrapher and a station agent before switching to sales work in the coal industry, and had become

C.L. Grigg was a founder of the Howdy Company, created in 1920 to promote the orange soft drink he had invented. When heavy competition led to slipping sales, Grigg decided to try something new. In 1929, he invented a lemon-lime soda and called it Seven-Up.

wealthy by investing in several mines. Grigg and Ridgway became friends, and in 1920 they created the Howdy Company, a firm based on Grigg's new orange drink, a few franchise agreements and a large debt. When St. Louis attorney Frank Y. Gladney prepared incorporation papers for the new business, he was impressed enough to join Grigg and Ridgway as co-founders of the company.[4] Born in Missouri in 1876, Gladney earned a bachelor's degree from the University of Missouri and a law degree from Columbia University. He had a private law prac-

tice in downtown St. Louis, and would remain as outside counsel to the company throughout his career.[5]

Ridgway and Gladney each invested $20,000 in the new company, while Grigg invested no capital, contributing only the Howdy formula and his marketing talent. All three men received 200 shares of stock. Gladney wanted to sell some of his shares to friends, but none were interested. Finally, he managed to unload 50 shares on Hugh Ferguson, founder of Columbia Electric Company. Gladney had successfully represented Columbia Electric in a patent infringement suit against the General Electric Company, winning a $250,000 judgment for Columbia Electric.[6]

Grigg and Ridgway rented a small office at the end of a long hallway in an area of St. Louis known as Bum's Row. Soon, it became crowded, and the company moved down the hall to larger quarters that included several windows overlooking the historic Old Court House, where the landmark Dred Scott decision had been handed down in 1857. Dred Scot was a St. Louis slave who sued for his freedom, arguing that he had lived in free states with his owner, Army surgeon John Emerson. But the court ruled that slaves were property, and belonged to people regardless of where they traveled. The decision, which also struck down the Missouri Compromise designating slave and free states, was a major catalyst leading to the Civil War.

Early Challenges

Both Grigg and Ridgway knew they needed to help their franchised bottlers promote Howdy. To guarantee quality, Grigg developed a small hydrometer, which he sent to bottlers for testing the sugar content of Howdy syrup. He also sent another hydrometer designed for testing bottler's stock solutions of citric acid, a critical flavoring agent.[7]

Grigg reminded his bottlers to "stick to the formula and fear no competition." He refused to take short cuts, believing that the superior taste of Howdy and his proven marketing abilities would win out.[8]

In the mid-1920s, one of Howdy's formidable competitors, Orange Crush,

Chapter VII: The Founding of Seven-Up

Above: The ledger of the Howdy Company, dated December 1920.

Right: A 1927 advertisement touting Howdy's use of orange oil. Grigg fought criticism by Orange Crush and others that Howdy wasn't flavored with orange pulp or juice.

bonated drink called Grape Bouquet, as well as a non-alcoholic "near beer" called Bevo. Generally speaking, breweries were not set up to bottle soft drinks, and efforts to convert them usually ended in failure. Grigg used existing soft drink bottlers instead of breweries.

Grigg introduced Howdy orange drink in clear 6½-ounce bottles. The idea of the 6½-ounce bottle was "borrowed" from Coca-Cola, whose deep green bottles announced the amount of beverage within. The popular Orange Crush was sold in 7-ounce amber bottles.[10]

By the mid-Twenties, Howdy had expanded to nearly 400 franchised bottlers. Unfortunately, Orange Crush continued to gain in popularity while Grigg's company still struggled to survive. Grigg and Ridgway realized something must be done to halt Howdy's slow but steady decline in sales and market share. They decided to formu-

began a nationwide sales campaign claiming any "orange soft drink" should contain a minimum percentage of orange pulp or orange juice. Orange Crush and other competitors stressed the "true orange flavor" of their drinks. At the same time, both state and national legislation were introduced that would require orange drinks to contain orange pulp or juice. The Howdy Company ignored this new trend, and Grigg characterized it as "a snare and a delusion." He pointed out that he was using a concentrate based on the essential oils of the orange peel, and had no intention of "making orange juice." He also noted that any so-called orange-juice product would require the addition of a preservative. He considered Howdy "the purest, finest most legitimate orange-flavored soft drink in America, period."[9]

The Howdy Company began during the time of Prohibition, and thousands of delivery trucks were sitting idle at closed breweries. Some beer companies tried selling sodas to stay in business. Anheuser-Busch, for example, produced a car-

C.L. Grigg wanted all bottlers to use 7-ounce green bottles, but his goal was difficult to achieve. Bottlers were allowed to substitute clear or amber glass if they could not find green ones. Uniformity of bottles was not achieved until 1950.

late an entirely new soft drink, to broaden their customer base.

In a 1979 interview, Ernestine "Dolly" Kiefer, daughter of Edmund Ridgway, described the reluctance her father and Grigg shared to shift their emphasis to a new product. "I can remember the days when Howdy was the most important thing in our lives," Kiefer wrote.

> "In the early Twenties the whole family — Dad, my mother, my brother and I — would drive to California in our 1921 Chandler sedan with jump-seats. The trip took three weeks. Keep in mind there were no interstate highways in those days, so we had three weeks of dust and bumps.
>
> "But the thing I recall most clearly was a huge sign on the back of our car that said 'Drink Howdy'. We brought along hundreds of small posters that said the same thing ... and we would stop frequently to stick them on fences and telephone poles. We had all been trained to act as ambassadors for Howdy. Howdy was the company in those days, and the company was my father's life."[11]

Despite their reservations, Grigg and Ridgway asked Warner-Jenkinson in 1927 to explore the creation of a new drink. They decided to avoid a new cola, root beer or ginger ale. They needed a fresh and new beverage. Assigned a key role in this task was Garret Meyer. In an interview many years later, Meyer said, "Almost every bottler in the country had some kind of lemon or lime drink, but there was no outstanding national brand that assured uniform quality. It was next to impossible to find a brand that was exactly the same from month to month. More importantly, you couldn't find one that had the same taste in Boston, Chicago and Seattle."[12]

Grigg reasoned that the addition of lithia to his new formula could do no harm and might attract some positive attention. Lithia is a naturally occurring substance found in minute quantities in bubbling waters fed by underground springs. Widely believed to have healing powers, it was considered an ingredient in ancient "fountain of youth" legends.

Trial extracts of a new lemon-lime flavor were developed in the late Twenties and sent to a number of Howdy franchise bottlers for reactions. The 11th sample seemed exactly right, and soon the replies came in unanimously enthusiastic about the new beverage.

Bib-Label Lithiated Lemon-Lime Soda

The Howdy Company's new drink made its debut in October 1929, two weeks before the stock market crash that ushered in the Great Depression. It was called Bib-Label Lithiated Lemon-Lime Soda, and it was formulated with 10 percent sugar (compared to almost 14 percent in Howdy) and was bottled with almost 90 percent carbonated water. The remaining ingredients were essence of lemon and lime oils, citric acid, sodium citrate for smoothness, and lithium citrate. Edward L. Taylor's bottling plant in St. Louis was the first to distribute the product.

It seems odd that the man who called his first two products Whistle and Howdy would saddle his new drink with such a difficult name. But C.L. Grigg wanted to capitalize on the lithi-

ated angle. Bib-label was included because Grigg intended to use paper labels, which could be dropped over the necks of otherwise unlabeled bottles like bibs to identify the new soft drink.

PAPARAZZI PHOTOGRAPHY STUDIO—
DR PEPPER/SEVEN-UP

Grigg wisely changed the name before significant damage was done. The drink next became 7UP Lithiated Lemon-Lime and then, simply, 7UP.

C.L. Grigg never explained how he came up with the cryptic name, though several theories have remained popular. Garret Meyer's three-volume history of the Warner-Jenkinson Company states that the 7UP trademark was selected because Grigg's first choice, Click, was already taken. According to one story, Grigg saw a cattle brand that resembled 7UP, and reasoned that if the mark was distinctive enough to help a rancher identify his cattle, it would be distinctive enough for a soft drink bottle.[13]

This theory is supported by the text of a speech that Frank Gladney delivered in 1942 to a regional meeting of 7UP bottlers in Kansas City. The text was located in the Seventies by Gladney's son-in-law, Ben Wells, the former 7UP president and chairman.

"He [Grigg] told me he had read an article in the magazine section of a Sunday newspaper on this history of cattle brands in the west. One of these brands consisted of the figure, 7, with the letter, u, at the top and to the right of that figure."[14]

Then there's the story about a dice game during which Grigg supposedly pleaded for the cubes to come *up* with a total of *seven* points. There is also a poker game story in which a seven "up card" was decisive. Even once the drink was established, people credited some of Grigg's own marketing with some sort of "reverse invention," as Grigg believed his new drink would cure mankind's "seven hangovers." And there's the story of "seven ingredients," and even the after-the-fact explanation that Seven-Up has seven letters. And, finally, the original 7UP bottles contained seven ounces.[15]

Regardless of the name's origin, partner Frank Gladney admitted he had serious reservations about Grigg's choice of 7UP as a trademark.

PAPARAZZI PHOTOGRAPHY STUDIO—
DR PEPPER/SEVEN-UP

"Once Mr. Grigg had made up his mind, I knew that further argument was useless.

"I was not only surprised but shocked. It seemed the height of absurdity to me to ruin the prospects by adopting the name of a common craps game.

"For at least a year or more I remained convinced that the adoption of it was a great mistake. I admitted that it was truly arbitrary and not even suggestive of a soft drink. Imagine my horror when within a few weeks Mr. Grigg had manufactured an enormous number of 7UP dice and began putting these out to the bottlers.

"It is not in daylight but in the dark that you see things that greatly concern you. After I had gone to bed at night and lay there in the dark, tossing under the covers, in my mind's eye I could see my money mixed up with those dice and both rolling away together. But, of course, I was woefully wrong and Mr. Grigg was entirely right. The trademark is one of the most perfect ever adopted."[16]

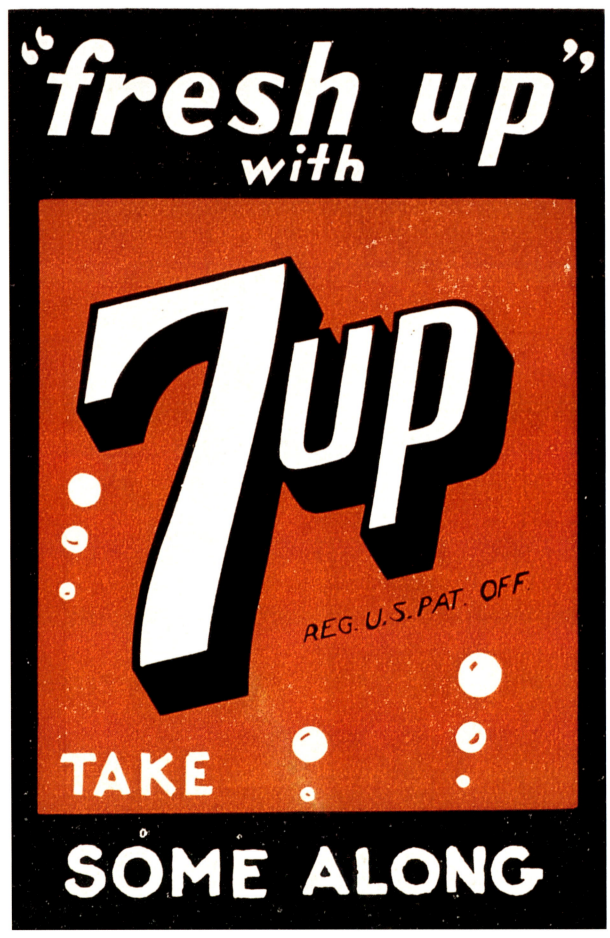

This 1936 advertisement uses Seven-Up's popular "Fresh Up with Seven-Up" campaign. Generated in the early Thirties, the slogan appeared on every bottle of the soft drink.

CHAPTER VIII
THE THIRTIES

"But how was business? Answer: perilous but always slightly improving."

— Dan Forrestal, describing
the early years of Seven-Up

ONLY TWO WEEKS following the introduction of 7UP, the stock market crashed and the Great Depression began. Thousands of banks failed and millions of people lost their jobs. While people stood in long bread lines and scavenged food for survival, it was not the easiest of jobs to sell a product made mostly of sugar and fizzy water. Yet C.L. Grigg remained confident. He continued to market his new lemon-lime drink as a premium product, refusing to compromise on price or quality.

At the time, Edward L. Taylor of St. Louis was the only 7UP franchised bottler. But Grigg and Edmund Ridgway convinced the Howdy franchised bottlers, who were struggling to stay in business, that 7UP was a potential gold mine. The entrepreneurs pointed out that 7UP was only 10 percent sugar, and sugar was the most expensive ingredient needed to convert the extract from St. Louis into sweet syrup before carbonation was added. Grigg spent considerable energy recruiting bottlers to package and promote his beverage. A handshake was good enough for him, but partners Gladney and Ridgway insisted on written contracts.

The Howdy Company, which had 17 full-time employees, relied on Edmund Ridgway to keep the books and on F.Y. Gladney, vice president, to act as legal adviser. Ridgway was responsible for moving the company in 1930 from the Granite Building in downtown St. Louis to the Cherry Blossom Building at 4545 Olive Street in midtown St. Louis. The building was the former home of a flavor company that had introduced a cherry drink in the Twenties, when many cherry and grape drinks were introduced and most failed.

Seven-Up's quality and consistency was best achieved in bottles, and Grigg refused to sell it as fountain syrup. Coca-Cola, Pepsi-Cola and other brands were sold as fountain syrups, ready to be mixed with carbonated water at drug stores, restaurants, and other places where soda was sold in a glass instead of a bottle. Grigg insisted on bottle sales only, and he further wanted bottlers to use a 7-ounce emerald green bottle. The green bottle criteria was not universally enforced because amber bottles were easier to obtain in some areas. Dr. B.C. Cole, who was hired as technical director in 1945, said it was not until 30 years later, in 1950, that the company achieved coast-to-coast use of the 7-ounce, emerald green bottle.[1]

Grigg might not have been able to get the green bottles he wanted, but he had four rigid commandments that his bottlers took seriously. They must charge retailers 80 cents for a case of 24 7-ounce bottles, they must "follow the formula and fear no competition," they must constantly recruit new customers through an aggressive sampling program, and they must have a label extolling the virtues of 7UP on every bottle sold.[2]

Grigg and Ridgway knew that many soft drinks were selling at 50 and 60 cents a case for 12-ounce bottles instead of 7UP's seven. They also knew that bottlers would be tempted to reduce costs by skimping on the most expensive ingredient, sugar. Grigg and Ridgway set up a national program to monitor quality control, and to stay ahead of competition, including a rival lemon product called "Three Centa."

Sales skyrocketed in the early Thirties. In 1934, 4,227 gallons of syrup were sold, a number that jumped to 9,036 the following year and an amazing 25,925 in 1936.[3] As the company continued to grow, Grigg decided to change the name to honor his star product. On October 2, 1936, the Howdy Company changed its name to the Seven-Up Company. By 1939, the franchises had expanded across the United States. Grigg could finally boast that 7UP could be purchased by every consumer in the nation.

Hamblett Grigg

In 1929, Grigg hired his only son, Hamblett Charles Grigg, known as H.C., to market the new drink. The senior Grigg needed someone to design advertising and labels, and give 7UP a

---

The Rise in Soda Consumption

Soda consumption has consistently risen in the United States, a trend that would lift sales of 7UP.

In 1849, the equivalent of 1 million cases of soft drinks were consumed, estimating a case as 24 12-ounce bottles. Measured another way, the average soda consumption per American was 1.1 bottles. In 1929, the year the first bottle of 7UP was sold, Americans consumed 181 million cases, or 35.4 bottles per person. By 1997, almost 3.25 billion cases of soft drinks had been sold, and a per capita consumption of 359 meant that the average consumption of every man, woman and child in America was more than one 12-ounce container of soda a day. In 1994, soda consumption climbed to an estimated 8.78 billion cases of soft drink, the equivalent of more than 536 12-ounce containers per person. Of total 1994 soft drink consumption, the equivalent of 255 million cases were 7UP, and 67.3 million were Diet 7UP.[4]

Above: H.C. Grigg studied to be an artist, but he joined his father's company out of a sense of duty. He was president of the Seven-Up Company from 1940 to 1965.

Right: C.L. Grigg argued that Seven-Up was slimming since it had less sugar and fewer calories than other soft drinks, easing hunger pangs until the next meal.

marketable personality. But Ham Grigg, 24, was not interested in the many details of business, preferring painting and art to commerce. Grigg had studied art at Washington University in St. Louis and had studied surrealistic and abstract art in Paris. During the Twenties, he put his artistic talent to commercial use designing several advertisements for Howdy orange soda.

By 1930, C.L. Grigg was nearly 62 years old. He was diagnosed with diabetes, and his sight was beginning to fail. Ham Grigg, swayed by a sense of duty, joined the Seven-Up business. In the early Thirties, Ham spent much of his time on the road, monitoring existing franchises or urging new bottling plants to introduce 7UP. He also designed labels, truck signs and point-of-purchase materials, and distributed advertising material for use by bottlers. He designed the first Seven-Up logo, with wings lifting the words.[5]

Advertising

In the early Thirties, sales promotion material was designed to entice both consumers and potential bottlers. Advertisements in newspapers, magazines and billboards were sponsored by independent bottlers, who could also use materials prepared at 7UP headquarters. "Fresh Up with 7UP" was a slogan generated at Seven-Up that appeared on every bottle and on cardboard and metal signs. "7UP—You Like It, It Likes You" was a popular advertising campaign in the Thirties. But the most famous of the early advertising was one recommending "7UP for 7 Hangovers." The specific hangovers that 7UP was supposed to cure were: overeating, underdrinking (the state of being parched), overworking, mental lassitude, overdrinking (too much illegal alcohol), overworry and oversmoking. This approach was conceived by C.L. Grigg and artistically illustrated by his son, H.C.[6]

Other appeals suggested that people consuming 7UP simply feel better. One advertisement claimed, "7UP alkalizes and corrects acid conditions. It normalizes and sweetens the stomach." Believing that carbonation had inherent health benefits, C.L. Grigg tried to convince customers that proper handling of 7UP was important. For many years, labels carried the message, "For the stomach's sake, do not stir or shake." Seven-Up should be slowly poured down the side of a tilted glass so the carbonation is not wasted, he claimed.[7]

Grigg called these slogans "selling ideas" and tried to include at least one in every letter or bulletin he sent to a 7UP bottler. Grigg's sales manuals were filled with advice and anecdotes. They included

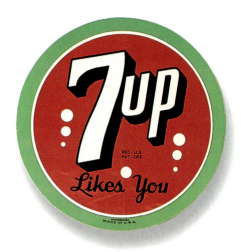

PAPARAZZI PHOTOGRAPHY STUDIO—DR PEPPER/SEVEN-UP

commentaries on "colored drinks vs. clear drinks," the dictionary definition of thirst, and the timeless advice for advertisers that "repetition builds reputation."[8] In the 1936 manual, he suggested that 7UP removes bad breath caused by liquor. C.L. Grigg also promoted the drink as a way to stay slim, noting that it contained 10 percent sugar, compared to 14 percent in the competition.

The End of Prohibition

When Prohibition was repealed near the end of 1933, the soft drink industry was temporarily shaken by the availability of alcoholic drink. Ginger ale had benefitted from Prohibition because it masked the flavor of low-quality illegal alcohol, and the drink remained popular as a mixer after Prohibition ended. C.L. Grigg saw an opportunity to market 7UP as a mixer. He also dusted off the seven hangovers claims. Sales

Early advertising featured the slogans, "7UP — You Like it, It Likes You," and "Fresh Up with 7UP." The advertising was generated at headquarters and used by bottling companies in regional marketing programs. National advertising would not begin until after World War II.

escalated. In 1934, 4,227 gallons of extract were sold to bottlers. In 1936, the number mushroomed to 25,925.

"A 1980 examination (good old hindsight!) of the company's various advertising themes indicates that stressing the mixer quality of 7UP went from hot to cold to hot to cold over the years."[9]

The "7 and 7" promotion, tied in with Seagram's 7 Crown whiskey, was one of the more successful campaigns.

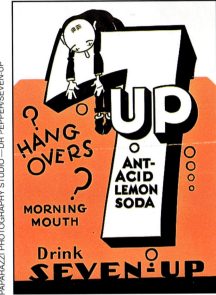 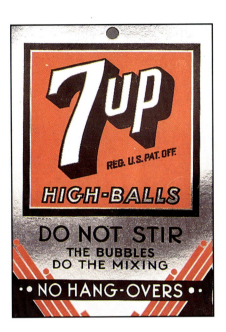

Left: After Prohibition, C.L. Grigg dusted off his claim that 7UP would cure seven kinds of hangovers. The company also began promoting Seven-Up as a good drink to mix with alcohol. The "7 and 7" campaign, tied in with Seagram's 7 Crown whiskey, was among the most successful.

Canada

Seven-Up established itself in Canada almost by accident. Bottler Max Gray of Winnipeg had heard about the lemon-lime drink manufactured in St. Louis, and wrote a letter to C.L. Grigg in 1934 requesting a franchise. The Seven-Up Company sent Gray the extract and advised him he could take over franchise rights for Manitoba.[10] Between 1935 and 1937, franchises were established in the Canadian cities of Winnipeg, Toronto, Edmonton, Calgary, Regina, Vancouver and the Maritimes. Though these bottlers sold a lot of soda, a crippling excise tax on extract and advertising from St. Louis made it difficult to make a profit.

Edmund Ridgway's son, Howard Eugene Ridgway, had studied engineering and economics at the University of Wisconsin, and was considered the perfect person to solve this problem. Ridgway established a Canadian subsidiary in 1938 called Dominion Seven-Up Company Limited, changed in the early Seventies to Seven-Up Canada Limited. Within a year, Canadian-made extract was available to Canadian bottlers, and the tax problem was solved.[11]

Though Ridgway returned to the United States in 1939, Seven-Up remained popular in Canada. By 1980, there were 70 franchised 7UP bottlers in Canada and 30 distribution warehouses. In fact, Saskatchewan was the site of one of Seven-Up's most embarrassing incidents. Clifford Andrew, packaging manager for more than 20 years, recalled the incident in a 1978 interview. Andrews had authorized a large billboard in the center of town proclaiming "7UP—Your Assurance of Quality." The painters completed the first two words and the first three letters of the third word before quitting for the day. The unintended message of the sign attracted the attention of newspapers and radio stations, and 7UP wound up with unexpected publicity.[12]

Seven-Up began a national advertising campaign during World War II, a move that paid off when the war ended and sugar restrictions were lifted.

Chapter IX
The H.C. Grigg Years

> "As president for 25 years, he guided, nay, pushed the progress of 7UP to its stature as the third largest selling soft drink in the world, and he built a strong organization of capable, enthusiastic people in the Seven-Up Company."
>
> — Ben Wells, on Ham Grigg

ON APRIL 16, 1940, at the age of 72, Charles Leiper Grigg died. Born in a tiny town in Missouri, he had made his mark in the big city of St. Louis, transforming fruit extracts into a successful business. When he died, a great void was left, and his unique talents would be greatly missed. In Frank Gladney's message to 7UP bottlers, he described a man who devoted himself to a product he believed in.

> *"To those of us who had a close-up view of C.L. Grigg at work during 20 years, the success of his efforts is not shrouded in mystery or attributable to good luck or mere chance. It was the natural result of his unvaunted but sterling ability, far-sightedness and patient industry.*
>
> *"His associates have no manner of doubt about the method, direction and range of his aspiration for the Seven-Up Company. They are keenly alive to the esteem and admiration in which he was held by large numbers of bottlers scattered all over the nation and beyond it. And they dedicate themselves unreservedly to the task of extending his work and ideals, or demonstrating to patrons of the company that they can and will build to new heights upon the solid foundation laid by him."*[1]

His son, Hamblett Charles Grigg, 35 years old, was the obvious choice to continue management of the company. Though Ham had always aspired to a career in art, he plunged into his new role with enthusiasm. A year earlier, Ham Grigg married Margaret Blanke, and even on their honeymoon, they drove around California, stopping in almost every city along the way to meet with bottlers and retailers.[2]

William Winter, who joined Seven-Up in 1946, and would later become president and chief executive officer, admired Grigg's enthusiasm for the business.

> *"He was very good from the standpoint of his bottler relationship and building the business. He personally operated out of his car before he was married, traveling around the country, calling on different bottlers and convincing them to take 7UP on."*[3]

Edmund Ridgway had died of a heart ailment in July 1939, so Frank Gladney, the last of the original founders still alive, moved from his role as outside counsel to become secretary-treasurer. Edmund Ridgway's son, Howard, returned from Canada and became vice president in charge of foreign business. "Howard took the international business and did a tremendous job getting 7UP started overseas," Winter said.[4]

Around the same time, a newcomer to the company brought fresh energy and insight. Ben H. Wells was a high school English teacher who met and married Frank Gladney's daughter,

PAPARAZZI PHOTOGRAPHY STUDIO—DR PEPPER/SEVEN-UP

The route drivers who delivered Seven-Up to local retail outlets were critical to the success of the company. They were the ones who distributed and marketed the product, and they were most in tune with the unique demands of their local market.

Katherine, in 1936. In 1938, Wells was lured out of the classroom and into the offices of the Seven-Up Company. He wrote copy for radio commercials, magazines, billboards and other materials for local bottlers. He later become president and CEO of the company, and Bill Winter remembered working closely with him.

"The real marketing direction for the business came from Wells. I may be biased because I worked closer with him and he was more of a sponsor for me than anyone else. He was really a very creative individual. A small man in stature, but he had a tremendous voice and he was an outstanding speaker. He'd travel the country, many days it was the state bottlers association meeting because he was in much demand as a speaker. A good sense of humor."[5]

Ben Wells, Howard Ridgway and H.C. Grigg, all related to the three original founders, advanced the company to a new level, Winter remembered.

"The three had totally different personalities. Each man in his own way contributed to the development of 7UP. Ben in his marketing expertise, Howard for administration and finance, and Ham for his leadership with 7UP bottlers.

"They didn't have anything in common other than the fact that through their families they got into the Seven-Up business. H.C. Grigg was in many ways a very demanding man to work with, yet at the same time was highly respected within the bottler organization. They knew he was a man of his word and whatever he said, well, that was going to get done."[6]

World War II

When the United States entered World War II in 1941, millions of men and women joined the military, and most that stayed behind worked toward the war effort. For the soft drink industry, war meant that sugar supplies were extremely limited, since the sweetener was pressed into service as a key component of explosives.

While most soft drink companies saw a drop in sales, Seven-Up continued to show gains. Since it required less sugar than most drinks, bottlers diverted their reduced sugar supplies from other

The company began a national advertising campaign during World War II, even though strict sugar rations meant that Seven-Up supply couldn't meet demand.

brands, and focused on 7UP, which was sold in 7-ounce containers rather than the usual 12-ounce size, further stretching sugar supplies.

In 1941, a technological breakthrough from Warner-Jenkinson made possible a double-strength extract, which permitted bottlers to use one ounce of extract instead of two to obtain one gallon of sugared syrup for 5.33 cases of bottled Seven-Up.[7]

During this period, advertising took on a national dimension. Bottlers were asked to contribute to a fund that would benefit them all by increasing product recognition and image. J. Walter Thompson, working on a project-fee basis, developed a national advertising plan, and in May 1943, bottlers were invited to St. Louis to ask questions and offer comments. Some bottlers wondered why the company wanted to increase advertising when the product was already outselling supply. The answer was that company executives wanted to position 7UP to take off once sugar rations were lifted. The bottlers voted overwhelmingly in favor of the plan, and agreed to contribute 2½ cents per case toward a national advertising campaign. The total appropriation was about $900,000 for May 1943 to May 1944. This compared to $6.2 million spent by Coke on national advertising, $1.3 million spent by Pepsi, and $1 million spent by Royal Crown in 1941.[8]

Uncle Sam pyramid cans were produced in 1970. One of the cans listed the sequence for stacking to reveal the face of Uncle Sam. There were fifty cans, each with information about a different state on the opposite side.

The national campaign was launched with ads placed in *Life*, *Collier's* and *The Saturday Evening Post*, beginning in 1943. Like many ads at the time, they focused on the war, urging readers to buy war bonds and drink 7UP. Patriotic themes were also displayed on billboards and point-of-purchase displays. The following year, 7UP ads appeared in 177 Sunday comic sections of newspapers.[9] The ads generally carried the same slogans and graphics that had been used in local markets.

A Sweet Dividend of Peace

When the war ended, Seven-Up was positioned to surge forward. The company had no sales force *per se*, but instead relied on bottler route drivers who delivered 7UP to convince new stores to stock it.

In 1946, William E. Winter joined the Seven-Up ranks in the important position of sales training instructor. Winter would become director of marketing in 1969, executive vice president in 1971, president and chief operating officer in 1974, CEO in 1976, and chairman in 1979.

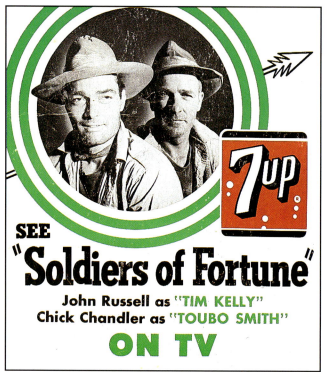

PAPARAZZI PHOTOGRAPHY STUDIO—DR PEPPER/SEVEN-UP

Above: The company increased national exposure by sponsoring radio and television programs.

Below: Seven-Up was one of the last of the great soft drinks to be sold in fountain form.

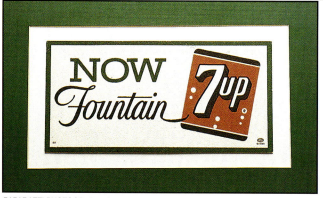

PAPARAZZI PHOTOGRAPHY STUDIO—DR PEPPER/SEVEN-UP

"Sugar rationing was still in effect when I joined the company in April 1946. Ben Wells had a lot of vision, a lot of foresight. He knew sugar rationing would be over soon. During the war years, there was no selling involved. You could just produce so many cases based on your sugar quota, and you in turn rationed it out to your customers. His whole premise was he wanted to set up sales training courses so 7UP bottlers would understand that you just didn't allocate the product, but you had to sell it."[10]

After the sugar rations were lifted, sales did not pick up right away. "Bear in mind that colas had a big share of the market," Winter said. "People, particularly in southern areas, couldn't get as much Coca-Cola as they wanted, and suddenly overnight, when colas became available products, then 7UP and some of the others suffered for three or four months. But after that, things got back into the swing of things."[11]

A brush with the Internal Revenue Service threw a scare into executives in 1944. The IRS claimed that the bottler cooperative advertising fund should count as income for the company, and therefore should be taxed retroactively, with 6 percent interest for both years the fund existed. The company argued that the contributions from bottlers went into a fund used for advertising to help the contributors. After many years of legal wrangling, the Tax Court of the United States announced in 1950 that Seven-Up did not have to pay the tax.[12]

The victory increased morale so much that the company began making plans to construct a $1 million headquarter building in St. Louis. On November 30, 1951, new headquarters were opened on the corner of Thirteenth Street and Delmar Boulevard.

International Expansion

Seven-Up began expanding outside the United States in 1948. The man who deserves the most credit for this move was Leslie R. Scott, a sales counselor who joined the company in 1942. He worked for Howard Ridgway, vice president in charge of foreign business, and when Ridgway was out of town, Scott often encountered requests for foreign franchises. He handled them on an individual basis, since the company had no system in place. When he proposed to Ridgway that the company formulate a policy for overseas franchises. Ridgway responded by putting Scott in charge of foreign franchising. For two years, Scott traveled from location to location, granting franchises, mainly in the Caribbean, Latin America and South America.[13]

On June 1, 1948, the Seven-Up Export Corporation opened for business in New York, with Scott as manager. At that time, there were 17 franchised bottlers in 11 countries besides the United States and Canada. In a 1978 interview, Chuck Thies, who became president of Seven-Up International, said Seven-Up was the third most popular soft drink in the world, adding that the company had 200 bottlers in 85 countries.[14]

The Fifties

In 1950, 7UP was the third most popular soft drink in the nation, with 104,488 gallons of extract sold each year. That year, the price of a gallon of extract increased from $38 to $55.50. The company had increased the price in lieu of asking bottlers to continue contributions to the cooperative advertising fund. The cost to bottlers was roughly the same, but the paperwork of administering the fund was eliminated.[15]

Seven-Up advertising began using television and radio, as well as magazines. Seven-Up sponsored "The Mark of Zorro" on television and "The Bert Lahr Show" on radio.

Around 1951, Seven-Up began working with dairy companies to create something called the "7UP Float." The relationship between the soft drink industry and the dairy companies had happily evolved since the 1920s, when dairy companies considered soft drink people mortal enemies. The 7UP Float increased sales of both ice cream and Seven-Up, by selling them together as a fizzy drink, flavored chocolate, vanilla or strawberry.[16]

In the early Fifties, Seven-Up responded to concerns from the Food and Drug Administration, and permanently removed the trace amounts of lithium from the formula.

New Packages

Between 1950 and 1960, 7UP began selling in vending machines, and was introduced in cans and non-returnable bottles. Seven-Up also sold for the first time as fountain syrup. The use of cans had been pioneered by the brewing industry, but the cans that held beer were inappropriate for soda, which was both more acidic and more carbonated. Flat-top cans of acceptable quality were introduced in 1953, but bottlers were reluctant to switch to cans because they had invested so heavily in bottling machinery. The cans, which were soldered together, could sometimes leak at the seams, and bottlers seized on this possibility as an excuse to stick with their trusty bottles.

Things changed in 1956, when a military base in Alaska said it would accept only canned soft drinks. The military business was too big to lose, and Seven-Up was soon offered in cans.[17]

In 1957, the Thornton Canning Company, which canned fruits and vegetables, decided to expand into soft drinks and joined forces with Seven-Up. The cans available in Alaska and California had flat tops and were opened with the pointed, triangular lever affectionately known as a church key. Later, a removable pull

Ben Wells was a high school English teacher when he married Frank Gladney's daughter, Katherine, in 1936. Within two years, he was lured out of the classroom and into Seven-Up, where he later became president and chief executive officer.

tab replaced the church key, followed by the ecologically superior pop-top.[18]

By the late Seventies, more than 40 percent of Seven-Up was sold in cans. Though cans are more expensive than bottles, customers prefer them because they are lightweight, easy to store and virtually unbreakable.

In 1961, 7UP became one of the last great soft drink companies to enter the fountain market. C.L. Grigg wanted to restrict the product to bottles, so he could guarantee the quality of every serving. Fountain drinks relied on soda personnel to add an often creative amount of syrup to carbonated water, so each drink could taste different. But by the early Sixties, new technology guaranteed that the soda would have consistent quality every time it was dispensed.

Company executives began winning fountain accounts from universities, fast food restaurants and other establishments where traditional sodas were sold, but they were most determined to win the McDonald's account. The giant fast food chain always refused, believing cola, orange and root beer provided sufficient choice. It wasn't until 1975, after Sugar-Free 7UP was introduced, that the company won permission from McDonald's headquarters to sell the product to individual franchises. All but 25 of McDonald's 3,000 outlets agreed to sell 7UP.[19]

A New President

On October 28, 1961, the last of the original founders, Frank Gladney, died. Ham Grigg was president, but for the first time, men not related to the founders occupied the top positions in the company. Daniel J. "Joe" O'Connell, the national sales manager, was named vice president and general sales manager, and Dr. B.C. Cole, technical director, was named vice president in charge of technical services and research.

In 1965, the Seven-Up Company began moving into a 100,000-square-foot building in St. Louis County it had purchased for $1.5 million. Around the same time, H.C. Grigg began searching for a successor. He was 60 years old, and had been president for 25 years. He had developed emphysema brought on by smoking five packs of cigarettes a day, and was mentally and physically exhausted. Two likely candidates for the job were the company's two vice presidents, Ben Wells and Howard Ridgway. Wells was the victor, largely because of a management strategy he had carefully mapped out that included an expanded management team with both increased responsibility and accountability. The Wells strategy included the appointment of four vice presidents. They were Robert W. Simpson, franchise director, William E. Winter, marketing manager, John T. Tabor, general counsel, and Joseph M. Thul, advertising director.

Wells became president on April 12, 1965, and Grigg became board chairman. Though he suffered from emphysema, Grigg still attended board meetings, often driving or being driven the single block to his office. Yet his influence was still considerable, as witnessed by his involvement with the introduction of Diet Seven-Up.

Bill Winter joined the Seven-Up Company in 1946 as a sales training person. He was president from 1974 to 1979.

Diet Seven-Up

Original 7UP, with less sugar than other sodas, had about 12 calories per fluid ounce, compared to 17 or 18 calories in other soft drinks. Yet in 1937, C.L. Grigg encouraged his St. Louis franchisee, Edward L. Taylor, to experiment with a non-caloric sweetener called saccharin. "At the time, Seven-Up was not considering the introduction of a sugar-free product for diabetics, though Grigg himself was a diabetic, nor for calorie-counting Americans."[20] Grigg wanted to know if saccharine could replace sugar in case of shortage or price increases. When sugar quotas were put in place, Grigg wrote to Taylor that saccharin should not be used unless sugar prices increased more than 20 or 25 cents a pound.

In 1953, the development of new artificial sweeteners prompted some soft drink companies to introduce sugarless drinks safe for diabetics. Diet-Rite was introduced by the Nehi Corporation of Columbus, Georgia, and No-Cal was introduced by Kirsch's Beverages, Inc., of Brooklyn. But 7UP dragged its feet, even when annual sales of diet soft drinks approached 5 million cases in 1957. Dr. B.C. Cole explained that the company was reluctant to market a compromise that didn't taste all that good. Ham Grigg, apparently, was reluctant to tamper with his father's successful product. Giving the same name to an inferior product would not be acceptable. "He would just say, '7UP is 7UP and that's it,'" recalled Winter.[21]

However, executives soon changed their minds after bottlers threatened to secure diet drinks elsewhere if 7UP would not provide them.

In 1963, Seven-Up offered a diet extract for a drink called Like. Before that name was approved, several others were considered, including "Datt," "Skip," and "Dis." Bill Winter remembers the difficult process of selecting the name.

> "H.C. Grigg could be a demanding man to work with. ... I know I was fired by him at least a dozen times when we were trying to introduce Diet 7UP, because he had made up his mind that he was not going to put the diet name on 7UP.
>
> "Every time we had any kind of meeting, and would bring it up, he would dismiss the proposal immediately. When we finally agreed the diet segment might amount to something and there

PAPARAZZI PHOTOGRAPHY STUDIO—DR PEPPER/SEVEN-UP

After much discussion, the new sugar-free formulation, introduced in 1963, was named Like. In 1973, the name was changed to Sugar Free 7UP, and in 1979 it became Diet 7UP.

> should be a diet drink from 7UP ... he came into a meeting and said, 'I've got two names and two advertising slogans.' One was called Skip, and had a corny advertising slogan. The whole idea of the slogan was to skip calories. But it was a very archaic kind of design. The other one he came in with was called DATT, an acronym for Diet Answer To Thirst."[22]

When Ham Grigg ultimately approved "Like," it received universal approval, and had the promise of great potential. The name was derived from an early 7UP theme: "You Like It, It Likes You." In 1969, the government banned cyclamates, and announced that sugar could be mixed with saccharin, a combination that was previously prohibited. Five days later, Seven-Up introduced a new Like with 3.5 calories per ounce. In 1973, the company took the next step and introduced Sugar Free Diet 7UP, later called Sugar Free 7UP, and in 1979 dubbed Diet 7UP. The Like trademark was later applied to a caffeine-free cola drink introduced by 7UP in 1982.

In 1977, saccharin, too, was found to cause tumors in rats that ingested enormous quanti-

Seven-Up has been such an enduring success that it has attracted dozens of imitators over the years. Here is a small sampling of the lemon-lime drinks produced worldwide that have tried to capitalize on Seven-Up's popularity and name recognition. All have failed.

ties, and the government announced plans to ban it. On November 23, the Saccharin Study Labeling Act was passed, postponing a ban that never actually went into effect.

Winter and Dr. Cole actually went behind Grigg's back to introduce Diet 7UP in 1969. "We had an executive meeting, and Cole and I made the presentation. We were so far down the line that he couldn't say 'no.' So we introduced the product and the design for the can. He wasn't exactly happy. But as soon as we came out with 7UP with the diet name on it, sales just went through the roof!"[23]

Changes

In 1967, Seven-Up went public for the first time. On February 16, 1967, 423,574 shares of Seven-Up stock went on sale for $22.50 a share. By the time Philip Morris Companies Inc. purchased the company in 1978, it had undergone two-for-one splits in 1969 and 1971, and each share sold for $48.

In 1969, directors of Seven-Up and Warner-Jenkinson, the sole supplier of extract, approved a merger. Under the terms, Seven-Up would be the surviving corporation, and Warner-Jenkinson would receive 74,905 shares of preferred stock.

Ham Grigg retired to the post of honorary board chairman in January 1972. He died October 24, 1977. A memo signed by Ben Wells described Grigg's profound influence on the company.

"When Mr. C.L. Grigg died in 1940, Ham became president of the company and carried on the principles of fairness in business dealings, utmost quality of product and unswerving, relentless promotion of 7UP and the 7UP idea. In arriving at business decisions, Ham's question was always, 'What is best for 7UP?'

"To some Ham seemed pugnacious — and he was a fighter for 7UP and what he knew was right. I say knew because Ham made no snap decisions. He turned questions over and over and in and out.

"Beneath the challenge that he often presented was a soft heart and a generous feeling for people. Only the many he befriended and helped knew the extent of that generosity, but it was great.

"As president for 25 years, he guided, nay, pushed the progress of 7UP to its stature as the third largest selling soft drink in the world, and he built a strong organization of capable, enthusiastic people in the Seven-Up Company."[24]

The "Wet and Wild" campaign, developed by the J. Walter Thompson agency, was the national campaign that preceded the famous Uncola campaign.

Chapter X
The Uncola

"I'd be a liar if I didn't tell you that my first reaction was that this doesn't make sense. The Uncola. What does it really mean?"

— Bill Winter

IN 1967, SEVEN-UP launched the now famous Uncola campaign and the impact was tremendous. The Uncola advertisements, featuring an upside down soda glass, succeeded in setting Seven-Up apart from other soft drinks, while reminding consumers that it is just as much an all-purpose drink as a cola.

"I always felt that the Uncola campaign that they launched in 1967 was the epitome of differentiation between themselves and the major colas," said Fran Mullin, president of 7UP until May 1995. "It was incredibly effective in building the 7UP user base over what they had been able to previously accomplish."[1]

The new slogan was the result of market research to analyze consumer perception of Seven-Up. Bill Winter, who was then vice president of marketing, explained the research process and how it led to the Uncola theme.

"One of the first things we did was set up an in-house marketing research group. We had three people in the department. Our first objective was to get a consumer view of what 7UP was. At the time, 7UP was the third largest selling soft drink brand in the United States, but we were surprised to discover that 7UP was not regarded as a soft drink by consumers. ... We put some interviewers on the streets in New York, Chicago and Los Angeles. There was no attempt to get a statistical sample, but you'd walk by and they'd say, 'Pardon me. We're doing a brief survey. Will you name for me five soft drinks.' Eighty percent of the time, 7UP would not be named. If they did not name 7UP, the next question was, 'Is 7UP a soft drink?' They said, 'Oh, yes.' So we did not have that kind of consumer recognition. ...

"Out of that, we came to the point of view that 7UP was the third largest brand, but it was not considered a soft drink the way colas were considered soft drinks. In many areas even today, Coke is generic for soft drink."[2]

Advertising executives at J. Walter Thompson brainstormed theme lines to address this perception. They thought about "the anti-cola" but decided it sounded too sinister, rejected "the non-cola" as too negative, then decided "the cola that isn't a cola" was too wordy. Finally, the magic phrase "The Uncola" was coined to describe 7UP. Bill Winter remembered his reaction.

"We were invited to see the presentation of the recommendation of the J. Walter Thompson account group. They came up with the suggestion of the Uncola. I'd be a liar if I didn't tell you that my first reaction was that this doesn't make sense. The Uncola. What does it really mean? Then we did focus group work and it rang a bell with consumers just for the fact that it was so different from anything else."[3]

Some of the bottlers didn't like the theme, perceiving it as negative advertising that could hurt their cola accounts. But the new campaign was clearly a winner. "We had 20 percent sales increases in April, with another 18 percent in May," Winter said.[4] The television advertisement featuring an "Uncola Nut" that is half lemon and half lime, and the deep voice of actor Geoffrey Holder is considered one of the best commercials ever.

New Packages

In 1971, the Plasti-Shield bottle, introduced by Owens-Corning Glass Company became a new vehicle for 7UP. The new bottle was a lighter glass, and it was unbreakable.

But an even more radical package was introduced in 1975, when Seven-Up was sold in one-liter bottles with the slogan, "Follow the Liter." It was the first soft drink to be sold in a metric unit, and it prompted a torrent of praise in the media. At this time, a national effort was under way to convert conventional measurement to the metric system. The Florida city of Pensacola, having recently gone metric, even changed its name to Pens-Uncola for a day in honor of the soft drink that had been a leader in metric conversion.

But the real reason 7UP went to the metric system had less to do with pioneering metric measurements and more to do with overcoming a marketing challenge. The company's technical staff had developed a new bottle shape that was less expensive to produce. Though it contained the same amount of liquid, it was not as tall as the old bottles. Executives worried that consumers would think the shorter bottles contained less liquid. The solution was to use a metric measurement, so the bottle actually contained more soda, and promote it heavily.[5]

In the late Seventies, 7UP's market share slipped from the 7 percent share it maintained consistently from 1970 to 1974, to 6 percent. Sugar Free 7UP steadily increased, from .1 percent of the market in 1970, to 1.2 percent in 1977.[6]

In 1976, Bill Winter, who had been president and chief operating officer since 1974, was elected chief executive officer. A year later, Hamblett C. Grigg died on October 24, 1977. Ham Grigg and his father ran the company for more than 35 years.

The year after Ham Grigg died, the family-run company was purchased by Philip Morris Companies Inc., a multi-national organization that was convinced it could double Seven-Up's market share.

The Takeover

Philip Morris Companies Inc. acquired the Seven-Up Company in June of 1978. The move was a surprise to executives at Seven-Up, but Philip Morris insisted it was not a hostile takeover. Seven-Up had been publicly traded since 1966, and was selling for $24 a share, Winter recalled. Philip Morris offered $30 or $32. Seven-Up executives resisted, and tried to find "white knights" to buy the company, including Kellogg, Warner Lambert and Colgate-Palmolive. "We were concerned about the beer affiliation, what little we knew about them," Winter said.[7] "They finally came in with an offer of $46 a share."[8]

"The interesting thing is that the three founding families still owned 51 percent of the company. It was spread out among a lot of people among those founding families. Some of them had no more interest in the 7UP business than the man in the moon, except as a stockholder. So they made pretty good money."[9]

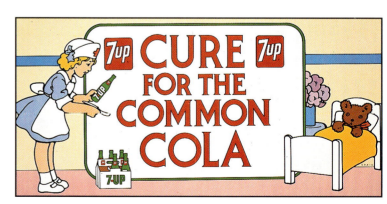

Though Seven-Up no longer made health claims, mothers everywhere gave it to children recovering from minor illnesses, like the flu.

 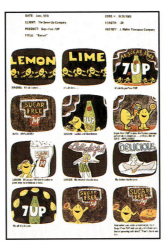  

PAPARAZZI PHOTOGRAPHY STUDIO—DR PEPPER/SEVEN-UP

From left: Eclectic advertising over the years included a return to the classic "Fresh Up" approach, as in this 1974 calendar, a Sugar Free 7UP television spot by J. Walter Thompson, "Feelin' 7UP" celebrity endorsements like boxer Sugar Ray Leonard and his son, Ray Jr., and the "Feels So Good Comin' Down!" campaign of 1986.

Philip Morris purchased the Seven-Up Company for $520 million. After the acquisition, Winter wrote a letter to "all 7UP Developers," confirming his confidence in the future of 7UP.

"We are looking forward with great expectations to joining the Philip Morris family. 7UP is now associated with a company that in 1977 ranked 28 in net income and number 52 in dollar sales in the Fortune 500. We are definitely with a big league company. It will be an adventure for all of us, and we are confident it will be the beginning of a bold new era for 7UP, 7UP developers and the Seven-Up Company."[10]

In addition to acquiring Seven-Up, the deal gave Philip Morris possession of Warner-Jenkinson, the company that had originally produced Howdy extract for C.L. Grigg, and had since grown to become one of the largest food color manufacturers in the nation. Winter remembered that it didn't remain intact for long.

"They didn't see any use for it, so they sold the color part of the manufacturing to Universal Foods in Milwaukee, Wisconsin, and then decided that they were going to build a state-of-the-art manufacturing facility for 7UP extract and Research and Development. So, they acquired this building. They spent somewhere between 12 and 13 million dollars just on this production facility."[11]

The new St. Louis facility would soon become a key element in the eventual merger of Seven-Up with Dr Pepper.

The multi-national Philip Morris organization had a reputation for acquiring companies, pumping money into them and turning their brands into top sellers, a strategy that had succeeded with Miller beer and Marlboro cigarettes. "They immediately said, 'We're so good, you know what we've done with Miller beer, taking it from the fourth beer up to number two," said John Albers, chairman and CEO of Dr Pepper/Seven-Up until March 1995. "They thought they could do the same thing in the soft drink business."[12]

The Philip Morris Years

Philip Morris appeared to have good intentions. In 1979, the company increased the 7UP advertising budget from $17 million to $40 million, equaling the amount spent by Pepsi to promote a drink with five times the market share.13 One of the company's first moves was to abandon the Uncola campaign that had worked wonders for the company since 1967 and switch from J. Walter Thompson Co. to N.W. Ayer & Son, Inc. "America's Turning 7UP" was the new theme, intended to position Seven-Up as a mainstream drink, not an alternative or special occasion beverage.14

Winter was named chairman of the board in 1979, and the company installed Ed Frantel, vice president of sales at Miller, as chief executive and president of 7UP. "He had been with Miller in the days when Miller Lite took off," said Robert Quirk, who began at 7UP the year following the takeover as area sales manager for New Orleans.15 Quirk moved up company ranks and in 1988 was promoted to senior vice president of sales for the Seven-Up Company.

But executives in 1995 agreed that Philip Morris did not fully understand the soft drink business. Winter, president of Seven-Up at the time of the takeover, said Philip Morris miscalculated.

> "They made a number of strategic mistakes, in my judgment. Number one, the lemon-lime segment of the total soft drink market has never exceeded 13 to 14 percent of the total market. It's dominated by colas. They thought that just by throwing money at the brand, and, I say this somewhat facetiously, using their renowned marketing expertise, they could jump that 14 percent — they could double it. ... You just don't change people's tastes like that. They did not understand the soft drink industry particularly, and the franchise company and the franchise bottler relationship."16

"They really didn't do their homework," Winter continued. "They knew 7UP was known nationally and had an internationally recognized trademark and they just thought they could do it."17 The problem was the assumption that selling beer was essentially the same as selling soda, said Francis Mullin, president of 7UP in 1995.

> "They elected to put some Miller beer executives in charge of 7UP and of course the mentality of a beer manufacturer working with beer distributors is not the same as a soft drink manufacturer working with franchisees. On the surface it doesn't look like there would be a huge difference, but when you look below the surface there are a lot of differences. But the beer industry never really fostered what in the soft drink industry became known as the parent company relationship that existed between a franchisee, who looked upon that franchisor as literally the parent company.

> "When Miller beer executives came in to run 7UP, their attitude was, 'Well, all you guys are supposed to do is distribute the product. And we'll market it and we'll tell you how to market it.' And that was anathema to bottlers. They just said, 'To hell with you. If that's the way it's going to be I'm going to devote my energy to other products in my portfolio because I don't have any faith in your

In 1979, Philip Morris dropped the Uncola campaign that had been so popular in the Sixties. The campaign was resumed after Philip Morris sold the company.

ability to do it without us collaborating about what's the best approach in my marketplace."[18]

Winter explained that losing bottler support has lasting repercussions.

"You don't lose franchises, but there was an adversarial relationship that was set up in many ways. For example, you go to the 7UP bottler here in St. Louis. He has Seven-Up, he has Dr Pepper, he has Squirt, he has Canada Dry, he has RC. So every time a representative of 7UP or Dr Pepper goes in there, he's fighting for the bottler's time and attention and marketing dollars. When you alienate those people, the attitude of some of

Cooking with Seven-Up

In 1965, Seven-Up published a recipe book called "Quick Recipe Favorites, Distinctively Different with 7UP," offering such treats as pancakes lightened by 7UP, or barbecue sauce enhanced by the lemon-lime taste.

Here is a selection of recipes from the 15-page book.

Sparkling Fruit Cup: Drain the juice from chilled canned fruit cocktail or fruits for salad. Pour chilled 7UP over the fruit just before serving.

Bacon Corn Crisps: Prepare one package corn muffin mix using 7UP for the liquid. Spread evenly in a well-greased jelly roll pan. Sprinkle with one small onion, chopped, and four slices of bacon, cooked and crumbled. Bake in a 375° F oven about 25 minutes. Cut in squares to serve.

7UP Braised Pork Chops: When braising pork chops, brown meat, then add 7UP and simmer gently until done. Gives excellent flavor.

Quick Basting Sauce: Combine equal amounts of 7UP and melted butter. Brush sauce on lamb shish-kabobs on grill.

Cherry Cloud Dessert: Dissolve one package (3 ounces) dark-cherry flavored gelatin in one cup boiling water. Stir in one bottle (7 ounces) 7UP. Chill until slightly thickened. Whip $\frac{1}{2}$ cup heavy cream. Stir in one-quarter teaspoon almond extract. Add thickened gelatin, mixing until well blended. Spoon into serving dishes and chill until firm. Makes four servings.[19]

Philip Morris spent nearly $13 million on the St. Louis production facility, which would later play an important role in the 1986 merger of Dr Pepper and Seven-Up.

them is, 'Well, if they don't appreciate what I'm doing, I'm just going to give my time and attention to one of my other brands. That's a lot of what happened.'"[20]

Philip Morris also alienated bottlers when it spent millions of dollars developing and promoting Like, a caffeine-free cola introduced in 1982. The new drink could not be sold by bottlers already selling Pepsi or Coke, as it represented a conflict for them. Quirk, then a salesman for 7UP, remembered that Philip Morris did not like to give control to the bottlers' sales force. "They just gave us programming," he said. "They were all national in focus. They just didn't fit all the markets."[21]

Even the successful 'Never Had It, Never Will' campaign, touting 7UP's lack of caffeine, alienated bottlers at first. Introduced in March 1982, the campaign highlighted the difference between 7UP and colas. However, it seemed to imply that caffeine was not healthy, and bottlers did not want a negative message attached to other drinks they handled. Bottlers eventually accepted the campaign when they saw how it boosted sales. "It was successful with the consumer despite the fact that in some cases the bottlers didn't want it," Quirk said. "Once the bottler saw that his 7UP brands were growing, and it really wasn't negatively impacting his caffeinated brands, he got behind it."[22]

There was no denying the success of the campaign, according to Winter.

"Things weren't going well from a growth standpoint, so they were looking for the hook that could be used to differentiate something. So they came up with this idea about caffeine — 'Never Had it, Never Will.' In many ways it was a hot button despite what everybody said. Coke has a no-caffeine version now, Dr Pepper has its no-caffeine version, and all the rest of them have it too. It did create some movement in the market, but at the same time it created problems with the Pepsi Cola bottlers that had 7UP, and the Coca-Cola bottlers who had 7UP, and even with some of the Dr Pepper bottlers. John Albers was with Dr Pepper at that time, as vice president of marketing, and he was very critical of the move."[23]

Quirk remembered that the no-caffeine strategy was an immediate success. "What really worked was that we made them aware that there was caffeine in the other products. ... If it was a clear product it probably didn't have caffeine, so it was better for you. Of course, it wasn't really."[24]

But Mullin said the strategy hurt bottler relations and prompted the cola companies to create caffeine-free colas.

"One of the biggest things that really shook up the bottlers was the fact that they didn't want to directly tell consumers that 7UP had no caffeine. And of course, Philip Morris latched on to the "Never Had it, Never Will," for a positioning foundation for the brand and incorporated it in all the advertising. It infuriated bottlers, even though there was an initial degree of sales success because they knew damn well that Coke and Pepsi were going to respond, and respond big time. And they did, by extending into caffeine-free."[25]

In 1986, Philip Morris sold the international rights for 7UP to PepsiCo for $246 million.

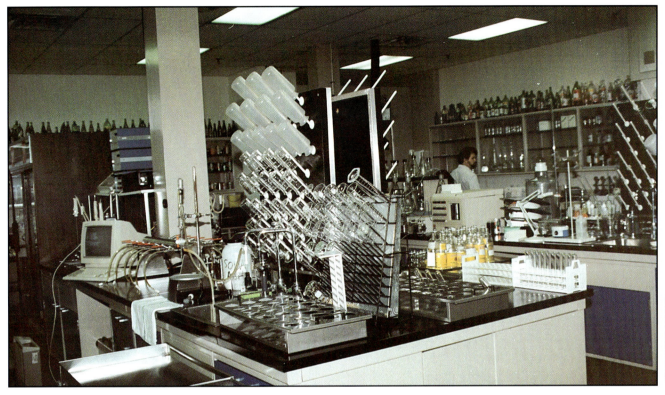

When Seven-Up and Dr Pepper joined forces, the state-of-the-art manufacturing facility near St. Louis was running at only 30 percent capacity.

For all the money it spent, Mullin said, Philip Morris damaged Seven-Up's strong market position. According to a 1982 article in *Beverage World*, 7UP in 1980 slipped in rank from third to America's fourth most popular soft drink.[26]

"Seven-Up was still quite strong prior to its acquisition by Philip Morris. And then, the seven or eight years under Philip Morris, a lot of things happened to work against the grain. ... It's a crime."[27]

By 1986, Philip Morris decided to cut its steady losses and sell Seven-Up. Pepsi offered to buy it for $360 million. The only problem was that the Federal Trade Commission (FTC) would not allow Seven-Up to sell the whole thing to Pepsi.

"Philip Morris only had one objective. Having decided strategically to get out of the soft drink business, they were determined to get out minimizing their loss. So, when the Federal Trade Commission stepped in and precluded Pepsi from completing its worldwide acquisition of 7UP, Philip Morris said, well, 'We'll still take your money for the international markets, and we'll try to sell 7UP to somebody else in the United States.'"[28]

In 1986, Philip Morris Companies Inc. sold the international portion of Seven-Up to PepsiCo Inc. for $246 million. Under the terms of the transaction, Pepsi owned the right to sell Seven-Up anywhere but the United States. All Philip Morris had to do was find a buyer for the domestic portion.

Spot was introduced in 1987 and rapidly developed into a popular cartoon character represented on 7UP packaging, clothing, and even as stuffed toys.

Chapter XI

Merging Dr Pepper and Seven-Up

"In all the years of the 7UP Company, from its origins in the Twenties, it pretty well paralleled Dr Pepper Company. In terms of market share and size, number of employees and number of bottlers, it was an absolutely parallel company."

— Jim Ball, senior vice president of corporate communications

IN AUGUST of 1986, the Dallas-based investment firm of Hicks & Haas led an investment group of equity owners, including Dr Pepper management to purchase Dr Pepper from Forstmann Little for $416 million. That October, Thomas Hicks and Robert Haas led an investment group of equity owners, including Dr Pepper management, to purchase Seven-Up from Philip Morris for $240 million. Combined with A&W Brands, Inc., which had been purchased in May 1986 for $75 million, Hicks & Haas then owned equity positions in three powerful soft drink companies. Together, the brands commanded roughly 14 percent of the domestic soft drink market and dominated the non-cola segment.[1]

The soft drink shake-up began earlier in 1986, when Pepsi Co made a bid for the Seven-Up Company then owned by Philip Morris. Jim Ball, vice president of corporate communications for Dr Pepper/Seven-Up, said the Coca-Cola Company responded with an offer to buy Dr Pepper.

"Within a week of the 7UP announcement, Coca-Cola, not to be outdone, stepped forward and said, 'We want to buy the Dr Pepper Company.' ...

"Coca-Cola people came into the Mockingbird headquarters, spent several months studying our company, reading our balance sheets, finding out about our employees and management. The Federal Trade Commission and Justice Department said, 'No, you can't do this. It's antitrust in its most violent form,' and killed both deals." [2]

Coca-Cola had been willing to pay $485 million for the company. Ira Rosenstein, executive vice president and chief financial officer of the Dr Pepper/Seven-Up Companies until May 1995, explained that once the deal fell through with Coca-Cola, "I spent the next 45 days running around the country shopping the corporation. We met with a number of conglomerates and major institutional investors and bottlers, and there was some interest, but nothing was coming together."[3] Eventually, investors Hicks & Haas stepped in. "We got to know Hicks & Haas when they were negotiating to buy our largest plant, the one at Irvine, for close to $95 million. I guess we gained their respect in that transaction and they came back and did a deal with us," Rosenstein continued.[4]

"Shortly thereafter, [CEO John] Albers learned that Philip Morris wanted to sell the rest of ailing Seven-Up, having already unloaded Seven-Up's international operations to PepsiCo. Seven-Up had a new concentrate plant and Dr Pepper needed more manufacturing space. Albers persuaded Hicks & Haas' Tom Hicks to help buy Seven-Up for Dr Pepper. The price for the lemon-lime soft drink line: $240 million." [5]

John R. Albers, who was already CEO of Dr Pepper, became CEO of Seven-Up as well. Seven-Up bottler James Harford was recruited to become president of the company.

The new group needed a brand to push, and that brand was Cherry 7UP. "Albers and Harford can't take credit for Cherry 7UP, which Philip Morris had developed," noted *Business Week*. "But they hurried the brand into national distribution without test-marketing it and rushed out effective black-and-white TV spots with pink accents."[6]

In early 1987, Seven-Up introduced Cherry 7UP and Diet Cherry 7UP. "Isn't it cool in pink!" was the advertising slogan. By the end of the year, *USA Today* and other national publications declared Cherry 7UP one of 1988's "in" new products. The American Marketing Association named Cherry 7UP one of the best new products of 1987.

"We sold 40 million to 50 million cases the first year," Albers said.[7] Also in 1987, Albers was named Beverage Industry Executive of the Year.[8]

According to Rosenstein, "The first-year sales of Cherry Seven-Up were 50 million cases, which was the largest new product introduction in the soft drink industry with the exception of Diet Coke."[9]

The first year after the merger, Seven-Up saw a profit of $30 million, Rosenstein said, adding that Seven-Up had rarely made money when it was owned by Philip Morris, and most years experienced a loss. "Our first year, we took it from 1985's $10 million loss to a $30 million profit. The first year we turned it around by $40 million."[10]

Despite these advances, Seven-Up lost the lemon-lime lead in 1986, when it was overtaken by rival Sprite, owned by Coca-Cola.[11]" I wish we still represented the bulk of the lemon-lime category, but the fact of the matter is, Sprite has done a very good job of building its business and it's a very, very tough competitor in the lemon-lime category."[12] Albers pointed out, "It's a little bit easier to be a product like Dr Pepper which has killed the competition, as opposed to Seven-Up, which has this big Sprite monster out there."[13]

Cherry 7UP was developed by Philip Morris, but the cleverly advertised product helped the Seven-Up Company turn around after it was purchased by a group of investors.

Introduced in 1988, Seven-Up Gold, a spicy caffeinated drink, did not survive a year.

"They [Coke] have done a very effective job with availability," Bill Winter remarked. "You walk into McDonald's and you'll find Dr Pepper because Mr. Pibb hasn't moved. But rather than 7UP, you'll find Sprite. You get on an airplane and ask for 7UP and you get Sprite."[14]

In 1988, Seven-Up Gold was introduced, "a spicy-citrus soft drink with caffeine,"[15] but the product did not survive a year.

Dr Pepper/Seven-Up

On May 19, 1988, Dr Pepper and Seven-Up officially joined forces to become the Dr Pepper/Seven-Up Companies, Inc. Two months later, the company moved its headquarters to Walnut Hill Lane, in Dallas. As Jim Ball remembered, enthusiasm was high.

"We had been operating as a merged company since November of 1986. The merger was more a financial reformation and had little effect on how we continued to operate. John [Albers] and Ira [Rosenstein] had already proven we could merge the two companies and be much stronger. We were growing the No. 1 and No. 2 non-cola brands with the best combination of bottlers to create the strongest dual bottling network in the business. As Coke and Pepsi were quickly buying up their bottlers, it enabled us to create a stronger position in the bottling community."[16]

Ira Rosenstein, chief financial officer until 1995, explained that Prudential Securities, a subsidiary of Prudential Insurance, was instrumental in creating the new company.

"Prudential Securities came along and wanted to make an investment in the company. ... They made a purchase of 49 percent of our company for $600 million, which sounded wonderful, but they only put up $100 million, and here we go with another $500 million of new debt.

"In 1988 when Prudential came in, we officially set up a holding company called Dr Pepper/Seven-Up Companies, Inc., with two operating subsidiaries, and we continued to go forward on that basis."[17]

Dr Pepper and Seven-Up were universally considered a near-perfect match. "It was a very quick transition," Ball said. "I think it was one of great discovery and awakening for [Dr Pepper] because we were acquiring a company of the same size as us."[18]

Pulling Together

Despite their similarities, Dr Pepper and Seven-Up differed in important ways. Ownership by Philip Morris had demoralized Seven-Up, while Dr Pepper was doing better than ever. "Seven-Up was a stepchild of Philip Morris and it was left out there with no direction," said Jim Gwaltney, the industrial psychologist hired by CEO John Albers to assist in merging the two organizations.[19]

"Dr Pepper has never been disassociated with its past. Dr Pepper has never lost contact with its roots. It's always been close to the living legacies. On the 7UP side, I've yet to meet anyone who knew who owned 7UP before Philip Morris.

"Dr Pepper was well organized, very practical, using a lot of down-to-earth sales principles, high contact with their customers, just seeing to it that they're regularly tending to business in what I consider a very down to earth way. Very close relationship with the bottlers. With the 7UP side, they just lacked direction."[20]

One of Gwaltney's techniques was to recommend a team-building, out-of-the-office program for executives.

"One of the things I recommended was an Outward Bound or similar experience. That would take these people out of the context of business philosophy and force them just to work in a mutually supportive manner. ... One of the first ones we did had mountain climbing, where they had to climb up a rock wall and you have two folks to depend on. ... For the second one, we took about 45 people, so it was not just the top level. We began to get the sales group involved. We did a desert trek, which was more demanding in terms of just survival."[21]

Fewer than 10 Seven-Up executives remained following the merger, Gwaltney recalled. "Dr Pepper essentially made the decision not to bring but very, very few of the upper-level managers into the system," he said, adding "they did for the most part keep the sales force intact."[22] Since sales staff worked principally in the field, merging with Dr Pepper was not a significant culture adjustment for them.

Saving Money

Merging Seven-Up and Dr Pepper provided an opportunity for both companies to work more efficiently. Among the reasons John Albers wanted to buy 7UP was that Dr Pepper needed a new concentrate plant, and 7UP owned a state-of-the-art facility that had excess capacity.

"When we acquired the Seven-Up Company and its concentrate plant, it was producing 700,000 gallons a year. We're now doing over 10 times that, or 9 million gallons, and we've only had to invest about a million dollars in capital improvements into the plant. That's a focus on production that turns directly into financial performance." [23]

Ira Rosenstein explained that the combined overhead of the two companies was less than the overhead of 7UP alone.

"Dr Pepper had general and administrative expenses of $12 million and ... Seven-Up's general and administrative expenses, which we never got our full hands around, ran somewhere between $27 to $30 million. We had a game plan that we would have the two operations' G&A at $24 million. ... That was done within 12 months."[24]

In addition to having less overhead, Albers suggested, the two companies were also more productive once combined.

"Seven-Up had not made any money from 1978 to 1986. I think the average during that time was a $2 or $3 million loss over each of those seven or eight years. They made as much as $1 or $2 million one year, but that's the extent of it. We sat down and wrote on a napkin and did all kinds of things, and I said, based on what their sales were, we could immediately make $30 million. That was my projection for the first year. To make a long story short, we made $40 million."[25]

Ira Rosenstein, chief financial officer until 1995, was a critical component in the financial success of Dr Pepper.

Dr Pepper/Seven-Up Companies moved its headquarters from Mockingbird Lane to Walnut Hill Lane in July 1988.

Different Marketing Strategies

Though the companies have long since merged successfully, they still maintain different marketing strategies. Dr Pepper pursues more of a national focus, while Seven-Up has been successful concentrating on more regionalized and local promotions, observed industrial psychologist Gwaltney.

"They [7UP] made a decision about three years ago that the attempt to spend heavy marketing dollars nationally was not paying off for them because they lacked cooperation and trust from the local bottler, and until they got that piece in place ... if the local bottler doesn't support you, you can have public out there who loves you, but you still don't get the product out there."[26]

Bottlers are essential to the success of a product since they are the ones who must distribute and market within their communities. James C. "Jimmy" Lee Jr., a long-time bottler in Birmingham, Alabama, told this story about how poor distribution hurts sales.

"I was in Jacksonville, Florida, in a Publix market and I noticed a woman, she looked like an employee, going up to two vending machines. They were side by side, and she looked around and in the Pepsi machine first and finally moved over to the Coca-Cola machine and bought a drink. I wondered what she bought and I went over there and she had bought a Sprite. The only reason she didn't buy 7UP was because it wasn't in the Pepsi machine. They had that Crystal [Pepsi] in there which isn't too good a seller anyhow. So by having that instead of 7UP, they lost a sale. Now, if that happens millions of times a year, it would cost somebody some money."[27]

Fran Mullin, president of Seven-Up from April 1991 to May 1995, said local marketing strategies are crucial to the success of the brand.

"There are lots of things that we have done that have implications of national umbrella support, like the basketball 7UP Shoot Out. But the real impact is all the things the bottlers are doing locally, either creating on their own or tying into things that we offer, as opposed to a national promotion where we have network TV support from time to time or the Shoot Out,

Above: These 1995 television commercials celebrate the bond between Dr Pepper and the people who drink it. In the "Part of Me" ad (left), Dr Pepper drinkers watch a fireworks display that ends with *Dr Pepper* spelled in the sky. In "Sign Man," (right), a highway worker uses his inventory of road signs to direct a Dr Pepper route driver to the edge of a cliff in order to get a Dr Pepper.

televised on ABC. That frankly has minimum contribution to our success. The real successes are the hundreds of local programs that are being created out in the fields and being executed by the bottlers."[28]

Reformulating Diet Dr Pepper

In 1991, the company reformulated Diet Dr Pepper, switching to an all-aspartame formula, and sales soared. True Knowles, then president of Dr Pepper, said before the formula was changed, the company conducted market research to discover what people wanted in a diet drink.

"They said they don't really like our diet drinks; they've had bad experiences with them. So, if you want to change your diet drink they don't care, whereas if you try to change regular Dr Pepper they'd shoot you. The second thing they said was, they'd like to have diet drinks taste more like our

regular drinks. ... So now all of a sudden we have a [diet] brand that tastes like regular, so we changed the packaging, changed the formula, said that new Diet Dr Pepper tastes more like regular Dr Pepper. ... So basically we can't tell you what Dr Pepper tastes like because it's a unique taste, but we can tell you that Diet Dr Pepper tastes like regular."[29]

The new formula was a remarkable success, Knowles said. "We doubled [sales] in '91, in '92 we grew like 25 percent, in 93 we grew double digit."[30] In 1995, John Clarke, senior vice president for marketing, said Diet Dr Pepper advertising would continue to focus on the taste-tested fact that Diet Dr Pepper tastes like regular Dr Pepper. "Tasting like a regular soft drink is the most important attribute consumers want in their diet drinks, and we've established this taste standard with Diet Dr Pepper," he said.[31]

Public Again

On January 27, 1993, Dr Pepper/Seven-Up Companies, Inc. went public. "Everybody on Wall Street in late '91, early '92, everybody and their uncle was going public. So we entered the fray, did our planning, chose our financial partners, started our road show," Ira Rosenstein said.[32]

"We've moved from a heavily leveraged private company to a stronger public company with a beginning equity of $15 per share," said True Knowles, president from 1990 to 1995, during the company's 1994 bottler meeting. "Our stock equity value, just since we've gone public, has grown roughly 60 percent."[33]

Knowles worked for 18 years at Procter and Gamble before joining Dr Pepper in 1982. He ran the food service business of Dr Pepper from 1982 to 1990. He took over responsibility for Premier in 1986, and the Dr Pepper bottle and can business in 1987. On October 25, 1990, he was promoted to president and chief operating officer of Dr Pepper Company, and was also named executive vice president of Dr Pepper/Seven-Up Companies, Inc.

Knowles is credited with having substantially improved and expanded the management of the company's food service division, making it the industry's second largest. By 1995, the division was selling to more than 120,000 food service and restaurant outlets across the United States. In the last five years of his tenure, Dr Pepper became the industry's

Spot, the animated red character that turned colas into the Uncola, boosted sales for Seven-Up.

fourth best-selling brand. All Dr Pepper brands grew 59.4 percent from 1990 to 1994,[34] while annual food service growth consistently scored in double digits. Those same years saw the Dr Pepper brands market share grow from 5.3 percent to 7 percent.[35]

John Albers, chairman of the board at the time, spoke with pride about Dr Pepper's success since going public.

"Together, we have made Dr Pepper the fourth best selling U.S. soft drink and the No.1 non-cola, with a growth rate exceeding the industry in each of the last eight years.

"Together, we have propelled Diet Dr Pepper to the position of the No.1 diet non-cola, growing three times faster than the diet category."[36]

True H. Knowles was in charge of Dr Pepper from the mid-Eighties to 1995, a period that saw its greatest growth in the second half of the 20th century.

New Advertising

Dr Pepper ads, created by New York-based Young & Rubicam, target consumers 12 to 34 years old. Dr Pepper continues to market itself as a drink unlike any other, and Clarke said years of marketing that message have paid off.

"You don't have to tell anybody in the United States of America that Dr Pepper is different. Everyone that is familiar with the brand, which is like 99 percent of the people in the U.S., know its taste, know the uniqueness of its taste and know the uniqueness of its personality as it has been developed through the 80s."[37]

The goal now, he said, is to position the drink so it stands out *in* the crowd, not apart from it. Clarke described the typical Dr Pepper consumer as someone who "drinks it because they are heavy soft drink users and cola may be their No. 1 flavor, but when it comes to an alternative, Dr Pepper is there, and Dr Pepper represents to them that uniqueness inherent in our personality."[38]

To help target these consumers, Dr Pepper uses coupons on the package, said John Clarke, senior vice president of marketing, giving customers a motivation to buy more Dr Pepper. The redemption rate is an industry leader, in the mid 20 percent range, he said.

"In knowing that the majority of our users are light to medium users where they drink Dr Pepper in addition to something else, we feel that it's a good vehicle for us to insulate and grow our light and medium user base."[39]

In 1994, Dr Pepper began a "Part of Me" campaign featuring a song by the same name. According to the company magazine, *ClockDial*, "Since the 'Part of Me' campaign went on air, 76 percent of consumers now say that Dr Pepper is a refreshing soft drink, a 4-point improvement from a year ago, and Dr Pepper improved to 71 percent on the sociability rating, an 11-point increase."[40]

Advertising in 1995 continues to focus on the theme of "tastes more like regular Dr Pepper." One television ad begins with a shot of a very technical-looking piece of equipment busily analyzing a glass of Diet Dr Pepper. A human hand takes the glass from the frame, and an announcer reminds viewers that neither human nor machine can taste the difference between Diet Dr Pepper and regular Dr Pepper.[41]

The food service division in 1995 continues to offer promotions and merchandising materials to support bottler efforts to build volume at every fountain location. Knowles said fast food restaurants sell a higher volume of soda when they offer Dr Pepper.

"Our drinkers are big drinkers. By that I mean, a Dr Pepper drinker, whether it be light, medium, or large, all are drinking over the national average of 46 gallons a year. They're probably in the 100 gallons. So they're big drinkers. When they walk in and see Dr Pepper, they order big drinks. I'll tell you, Mr. Foodservice Operator, when you put Dr Pepper in your establishment, it's not going to bring one more customer, but when they come in, they're going to sell more ounces and you're going to make more money."[42]

Once Philip Morris divested the domestic rights to 7UP brands, the new management began an aggressive strategy to regain market share. Two ad campaigns were instrumental in turning the company around. One was the "Never Had it, Never Will" concept touting Seven-Up's lack of caffeine, and the other was Spot, the ultra-cool, red animated creature featured in so many commercials and print ads. Spot was introduced in 1987, and rapidly developed into a popular cartoon character represented on 7UP packaging, clothing and even as stuffed toys, Mullin said.

"There were people who were very enthusiastic at the bottler level about Spot. There were people who were very, very unenthusiastic and against the use of Spot in our marketing plan. Today I'd say again there are always a few out there who aren't really happy, but Spot is still an integral part of our communications strategy. Most of our bottlers now understand how Spot is being used and agree with that usage as a facilitator, to facilitate the transformation from a cola to 7UP the Uncola."[43]

National marketing strategies for 7UP include tie-ins with popular, regional sporting events, such as a golf tournament in Tyler, Texas, for

Spot was an instant marketing success for 7UP, and has appeared on clothes, as stuffed animals, and even as telephones.

example. The company has considered sponsoring a car in NASCAR, but "we just haven't found ourselves at that point yet," Clarke said. "I'd rather spend the money saying something about the product."[44]

"There is such a high level of enthusiasm out in the market place right now for 7UP," said Fran Mullin, president until May 1995. "Everybody seems to be operating in sync these days."[45]

"I'm fortunate to have worked with people who are incredibly motivated, they're seeing the results of their labors. They're the very same people who were frustrated, discouraged and scratching their heads, trying to figure out how in the world they were ever going to stop the flow of volume losses and share losses. Now they are growing their business for the third year in a row."[46]

One of a series of paintings by W.H. Barribal, created in 1919 for Schweppes advertising.

Chapter XII
Cadbury Schweppes

"I knew Dr Pepper was something very unusual and special, and as far as I was concerned, we could not go wrong being involved with Dr Pepper."

— Chairman Dominic Cadbury,
of Cadbury Schweppes plc

ON MARCH 2, 1995, Cadbury Beverages, the beverage division of Cadbury Schweppes plc, purchased the Dr Pepper/Seven-Up Corporation for $1.7 billion, (plus about $870 million of Dr Pepper/Seven-Up debt) fulfilling its goal of becoming the largest non-cola soft drink company in the world. The combined companies command more than half of the United States non-cola market, and 17 percent of the total U.S. soft drink market, making it the third-largest soft drink company in the world, behind Coke and Pepsi. "One company has never owned so many brands," said John Brock, president of Dr Pepper/Cadbury North America.[1]

Schweppes

Jean Jacob Schweppe founded the company that bears his name in 1783. Though a jeweler by trade, he had an interest in science, and in his spare time he studied the novel art of infusing water with oxygen. He eventually became so fascinated with this new science that he pursued it full time. As he experimented, he gave away the bubbling water that he created. Eventually, Schweppe began charging a small fee for the water to cover his expenses, and that's how the company was born.[2]

Schweppe founded the world's first carbonated beverage establishment in Switzerland, then moved it to London in 1792. Artificial mineral waters were not new when Schweppe arrived, but his products were superior to others, due to the proprietary compression pump method he employed.[3] He died in 1821, at the age of 81. According to *Schweppes*, a book written on the 200th anniversary of the company, Schweppe created a new standard for carbonation.

"By his ingenuity and determination 20 years before, Jacob had transformed both the quality and scale of production of artificial mineral waters. ... Transplanted in England, that commerce had, from small and precarious beginnings, flourished exceedingly, inspired by his genius. He now left his incomparable name and reputation in the hands of his successors."[4]

Those successors helped Schweppes thrive for more than two centuries. In 1835, the partners introduced Schweppes Aerated Lemonade, a new direction for a company that had sold only soda water and artificial mineral water for more than 50 years. In May 1865, production of Schweppes was taken north of England for the first time, with the opening of a factory in Glasgow, Scotland. In 1877, a plant was opened in Sydney, Australia, and in 1884, Brooklyn, New York became the home of a Schweppes factory. During the 1870s, tonic water and ginger ale were introduced, as well as a cola beverage.

J. Schweppe & Company Ltd. was incorporated on January 2, 1893, and the newly structured company continued to grow. Schweppes began selling fruit juices in 1907, when it marketed a non-alcoholic wine called Vin de Vie. In December 1909, Schweppes began bottling its own lime juice. The company continued to introduce new products, including Sparking Grape Fruit and Sparkling Lemon in 1932, and the highly successful Bitter Lemon in 1957.

Schweppes was growing overseas, but it needed more financial muscle to compete in foreign markets. Company executives began looking for a company with which it could merge, strengthening the assets of both.

Cadbury

In 1824, John Cadbury opened a grocery store in Birmingham, England. In addition to food and household staples, he sold cocoa and drinking chocolate, prepared by hand with a mortar and pestle. When the business expanded to a warehouse in 1831, Cadbury began manufacturing drinking chocolate and cocoas. In 1847, the business moved again to a larger factory, and John Cadbury brought his brother, Benjamin, in as a partner. In 1853, Cadbury Brothers received the Royal Warrant as manufacturers to Queen Victoria, and to this day the company continues to hold Royal Warrants of Appointment.

John Cadbury retired in 1861 and his two sons, Richard and George, continued the enterprise. They struggled to make a living for the first five years, with barely enough customers to keep the business afloat. Dissatisfied with the quality of products produced by all manufacturers, including their own, the brothers took a momentous step in 1866 — they introduced a process that pressed cocoa butter from cocoa beans, producing cocoa essence, forerunner of the cocoa we know today. The plentiful supply of cocoa butter remaining after the cocoa was pressed made it possible to manufacture a wide variety of confectionery chocolates. From the mid 1860s onward, Cadbury's introduced many varieties of chocolate products, from plain bars to fancy tidbits filled with flavored creams.

The company continued to grow, expanding overseas to Australia, New Zealand, South Africa, the West Indies, South America, the United States and Canada. In 1899, it became a private limited company, called Cadbury Brothers Ltd.

Dairy Milk, the most popular molded chocolate in the United Kingdom, was introduced in 1905. Produced as a direct challenge to the milk

Above: Jean Jacob Schweppe was a jeweler by trade, but his interest in the novel art of carbonating water led him, in 1783, to found the company that bears his name. For more than two centuries, Schweppes has been a leader in the soft drink industry.

Right: Schweppes' Seltzer Water set new standards of quality for carbonated beverages.

chocolates from France and Switzerland, George Cadbury Jr. spent a considerable amount of time and money developing it. In 1919, Cadbury Brothers merged with J.S. Fry & Sons of Bristol, whose products included Turkish Delight and Fry's Chocolate Cream.

Cadbury today is a high-tech company with plants capable of making and wrapping 800 bars a minute. These systems also assure product uniformity, and that fruits and nuts, when added, were evenly distributed. Members of the Cadbury family remain involved to the present day, and the chairman of the company is Dominic Cadbury.

The Merging of Cadbury and Schweppes

While Schweppes searched in the late Sixties for a global business partner, Cadbury had similar goals. Its chocolate sold well, but it lacked the muscle to fight overseas competitors. At a 1968 marketing conference in London, representatives of both companies spoke about the future they desired for their respective companies.

"Having listened to one another's contribution on overseas and home marketing, they were struck by the similarity of approach of both their companies. This led to informal talks on scope for collaboration at home and abroad. The discussions brought a growing conviction that each company had much to offer the other, and that a merger of their operations would result in the creation of a strong international group ranking high among world companies. As the talks went on, both companies felt increasingly confident that in the future they could make more profits together than separately." [5]

Schweppes advertisements frequently play on the sound of the word, referring to a feeling of "Schweppervescence" and a mythical county of "Schweppshire." This 1940 ad is a classic example of onomatopoeia.

Schweppes and Cadbury merged in 1969. The company has two product "streams," each with its own management structure—the beverages stream, called Cadbury Beverages, and the confectionery stream. Today, Cadbury Schweppes is an international group of companies with more than 39,000 employees.

Since 1985, the company has acquired a number of prestigious soft drink brands, said John Brock, president of Cadbury Beverages North America, who now shares responsibility for the combined group.

"In 1985, our business in the U.S. was comprised of Schweppes. We had 22 million 12-ounce cases with about .5 percent share of the U.S. soft drink market. Our business has grown significantly over the years. In 1986 we purchased Canada Dry and Sunkist soft drinks from the R.J. Reynolds Company. This gave us an additional 100 million cases and increased our market share to about 3 percent. Then in 1989 we followed this with the acquisition of Crush and Hires from the Procter and Gamble Company for an additional 18 million cases, and about .5 percent increase in market share. Then in 1993, about 18 months ago, we acquired A&W, Squirt and Vernor's. That added an additional 1.8 percent market share, bringing the total to something over 5 percent." [6]

The company recently introduced Crystal Light Diet soft drink and Hershey's Chocolate soft drink.

The Acquisition

Cadbury Schweppes' interest in Dr Pepper began in 1986, when it participated in the Hicks & Haas leveraged buyout of Dr Pepper from Forstmann Little. Dominic Cadbury, chairman of Cadbury Schweppes, said the whole thing began almost by accident, when Cadbury officials were doing business with Shearson Lehman Brothers, who were involved in the Dr Pepper transaction.

"Our chief financial officer was visiting in New York at the time, and he was visiting Shearson Lehman. ... There were some gentlemen upstairs, Bobby Haas and Tom Hicks, and they were involved in putting together another leveraged buyout of the Dr Pepper business. That was interesting to chew because we had this small soft drink business in the United States, and we were always looking to expand it. ... One thing led to another very quickly, and we agreed that we would be part of that leveraged buyout.

Richard (left) and George Cadbury (right) took over the family business when their father, John Cadbury, retired in 1861.

"I was in fact on holiday with my family at a Club Med resort in Turkey, and wasn't expecting to get a phone call from anybody. But anyway, I got this phone call saying we had the opportunity to share in this buyout and from memory, I think the price was around $11.6 million. Having spent time in the states, I knew Dr Pepper was something very unusual and special, and as far as I was concerned, we could not go wrong being involved with Dr Pepper."[7]

Cadbury contributed roughly 30 percent of the $35 million equity toward the $416 million buyout, which took place the same year Hicks & Haas purchased Seven-Up and A&W. Since Cadbury had made such a substantial investment, it seemed likely that the company would acquire even more of Dr Pepper over time, Cadbury explained.

"It just seemed to me that if you were going to be involved in a 30 percent share of the equity that ...

*we had a good chance of increasing that over time because we were the only industry participant. All the rest of the participants in the buyout were financial houses, and it seemed to me that the financial participants were bound to want to turn their investment over at some point and move on to other things. It seemed to me very likely that at some point in the future we would have the opportunity to raise our share."*⁸

That opportunity came in 1993. Prudential Securities, which had purchased 49 percent of Dr Pepper/Seven-Up in 1988 for $100 million, had reduced its shares to 20.2 percent. When Prudential elected to sell its remaining shares, Cadbury bought them, increasing its holdings of Dr Pepper/ Seven-Up from 5.7 percent to 25.9 percent.

Cadbury Schweppes' 1993 Annual Report explained that the investment was good for Cadbury because "Dr Pepper/Seven-Up manufactures much of the concentrate for our brands in the U.S. market, and in addition, certain of our brands are sold by Dr Pepper/Seven-Up in the food service sector."⁹

Frank Swan, managing director of Cadbury Beverages Stream, said, "We identified a few years ago that we wanted to be the number one non-cola soft drink company in the world. ... So we set out to have a look at what might fit with our business in the United States, and quite clearly operations like A&W and ultimately Dr Pepper/Seven-Up came to the fore."¹⁰

According to *Barron's*, "Albers was angry that Pru sold its stake to Cadbury, but, as he told a Dallas paper, 'There wasn't a damn thing we could do about it.' There was, however, something he could do to hold Cadbury at bay, and he did it. Within days, in a classic knee-jerk reaction, Dr Pepper refused Cadbury any board representation."¹¹

Albers also felt that a Cadbury board seat would create a conflict of interest and compromise proprietary information, since the companies sold competing root beers, with Dr Pepper producing IBC Root Beer and Cadbury selling both A&W and Hires.

The *Barron's* article, written in 1993, noted that it seemed inevitable that Cadbury would attempt to purchase Dr Pepper.

"Dr Pepper already manufactures soft drink concentrates for Cadbury at an efficient plant near St. Louis, and the two companies' networks of bottlers overlaps considerably, offering

Formulated in 1905 to compete with Swiss milk chocolates, Cadbury Dairy Milk was briefly known as Dairymaid. The delightful advertisement above emphasizes the fresh milk that was incorporated in the successful recipe.

*numerous possibilities for cost savings. Furthermore, with foreign sales now accounting for a minuscule part of Dr Pepper's revenues, Cadbury is particularly interested in taking the brand international."*¹²

In a 1994 interview not long before a Cadbury Schweppes offer was tendered, John Albers, then Dr Pepper chairman, said he would take an offer from Cadbury seriously.

*"If it were a bona fide offer, I'd have a fiduciary responsibility to our shareholders. I'm not like some of those CEOs who fight to hold their jobs. I'm gone tomorrow. I've done my job building the brands to where they are worth a lot more money."*¹³

Cadbury Beverages brands include Dr Pepper, Seven-Up, Welch's, IBC Root Beer, Canada Dry, Schweppes, A&W, Crush, Sunkist, Squirt, Mott's, Hires, Sun-drop, Vernor's Country Time, Naya, Crystal Light and Hershey's. The company sells more than half of the non-cola soft drinks in the United States.

Dominic Cadbury, chairman of Cadbury Schweppes plc, now heads the largest non-cola soft drink company in the world. Before becoming chairman in 1993, he served as group chief executive since 1983.

The World's Largest Non-Cola Company

The inevitable happened January 26, 1995, when Cadbury Schweppes tendered an offer to buy all the outstanding shares of Dr Pepper at $33 a share, for a total of $1.7 billion. The transaction was approved by the Federal Trade Commission on February 16, and it became official March 2 when Cadbury Schweppes acquired more than 90 percent of the outstanding shares of Dr Pepper/Seven-Up Companies, Inc.

Between 1984 and 1995, Dr Pepper/Seven-Up increased shareholder value by almost $2.7 billion., as Chief Financial Officer Ira Rosenstein led the company in more than $9.7 billion in financial transactions.

Dominic Cadbury said the new company represents more than 50 percent of the non-cola segment of the market. "We acquired the business with the intention of creating a bigger alternative force in the market, a market share somewhere between 16 and 17 percent. That's a very significant force."[14]

As the largest non-cola soft drink company in the world, Cadbury commands a growing market. "Growth of these drinks is far outpacing growth of cola sales," according to a *Barron's* article, "much to the chagrin of Coke and Pepsi, which are now commonly referred to in the soda trade as victims of 'cola fatigue.'"[15]

The new organization is led by John Brock, president and CEO of an enlarged Cadbury Beverages enterprise. In April, the new company was named Dr Pepper/ Cadbury North America (DPCNA) and reformed into three operating entities: Dr Pepper USA, comprised of Dr Pepper brands sold in bottles and cans; Dr Pepper Foodservice, representing all corporate fountain drinks; and Cadbury Beverages North America, a three-tier division comprised of 7UP brands and all Cadbury brands except Dr Pepper.

In March 1995, Brock declared that he would reform the company under a "best-person, best-job" scenario, a task that took slightly more than 90 days. "John [Brock] has been working night and day," John Albers said, "to understand the culture of our company and formulate a plan of consolidation to maximize the productivity and profitability of the new company."[16]

Brock, a chemical engineer from Georgia Tech, worked with Procter and Gamble for 11 years. In 1983, he became vice president of technical and operations for Cadbury Beverages North America, and became president of the international soft drink business in 1990. In 1990, he was named president of Cadbury Beverages Europe and in 1993 became president of Cadbury Beverages North America.[17]

In May 1995, Albers, Rosenstein, Knowles and Mullin left the company to pursue other interests. Dr Pepper senior managers Jack M. Kilduff and Gil Cassagne were promoted to chief operating officers of Dr Pepper USA and Foodservice respectively. Todd Stitzer, who led A&W during its recent growth years, was named chief operating officer of Cadbury Beverages North America (CBNA). This unit is led by Peter Wurzer of Cadbury Beverages, and Mike McGrath and Rick Wach of Dr Pepper/Seven-Up. McGrath had successfully managed the company's Welch's and IBC Root Beer business, while Wach was vice president of marketing of the Dr Pepper/Seven-Up Foodservice Group.

"If there is any single thing to describe how we plan to manage the Dr Pepper business in the United States, it's that we intend to keep doing all the things that seem to be working so effectively. For example, the headquarters of Dr Pepper is going to remain in Texas. We are keeping the organizational structure of Dr Pepper, both the bottle and can business, and the fountain food service business, just like it has been. Bottler relationships are so important, and everything we see and hear says there is a very special relationship between Dr Pepper bottlers and Dr Pepper management, and the entire Dr Pepper field sales organization. We plan to do everything possible to keep that just as it has been."[18]

Seventy-five percent of Dr Pepper is bottled by Coke and Pepsi bottlers that do not have a competing product in the pepper-type category, Brock said. He described Dr Pepper as "a Texas institution with the structure in place and a family-like relationship with bottlers."[19]

"Seven-Up, Welch's and IBC are outstanding brands which will be combined with the existing Cadbury Beverages business in Stamford," Brock observed. "Our objective for this new business unit will be to lead non-cola category growth with revitalized Seven-Up as the driver."[20]

Bigger and Stronger

The merger brought Dr Pepper, Seven-Up, Welch's and IBC Root Beer together with Canada Dry, Schweppes, A&W, Crush, Sunkist, and Squirt. A transition team of existing Cadbury and Dr Pepper management personnel was successful in putting together the CBNA group following exhaustive study and tireless work in Stamford and Dallas.

According to *Barron's*, critical mass is vital in the soft drink industry. "An enlarged Cadbury would be in a position to offer bottlers a strong stable of high-margin non-cola brands," said a 1993 article. "As a result, it would demand better store displays, better promotions and better terms."[21]

Beverage Industry magazine discussed another aspect of critical mass in its 1994 Annual Soft Drink Report.

"Because Cadbury Schweppes is acquiring two top national brands (when it had none of its own), and because these two brands (Dr Pepper and 7UP) are largely distributed by the Coca-Cola and Pepsi-Cola bottling system, the majority of Cadbury revenues will come from bottlers whose primary business is selling Coke and Pepsi products.

"The question some are asking is, for the sake of short-term critical mass, has Cadbury played into

Above left: Hershey's Chocolate Drink is among the most recently introduced products sold by Cadbury Schweppes.

Below: Cadbury's Dairy Milk, formulated in 1905, is today the No. 1 molded chocolate in the United Kingdom.

John F. Brock, president of Cadbury Beverages North America since 1993, and the new leader of Dr Pepper/Cadbury North America.

the hands of Coke and Pepsi and the influence they can exert through their bottling systems?"[22]

Frank Swan, managing director of the Cadbury Beverages Stream, said Cadbury is positioned to challenge industry leaders Coca-Cola and PepsiCo. "I am duly respectful of their size and ability," he said in a 1993 *Barron's* article. "But I'm not frightened. We have been in this end of the business longer than they have and we know it better. I think we can be faster on our feet than Coke and Pepsi."[23]

Brock noted that Coke commands 41 percent of the soft drink industry and Pepsi has 32 percent. "While Coke and Pepsi each have their cola giants, their mega brands, we actually have the preferred portfolio in non-cola," he said. "That's what we really bring to the party. Our brands are the No. 1 or No. 2 national brands in their category, or they are regional powerhouses like Sun-drop in North Carolina and Vernor's in Michigan."[24]

Following the merger, Swan explained the strength of the worldwide Cadbury Schweppes organization to a meeting of Dr Pepper/Seven-Up employees in Dallas.

"Cadbury Schweppes is a company which operates in the beverage and confectionery markets globally. Our worldwide headquarters are in London. We employ over 39,000 people worldwide. Our quality brands have been bought and enjoyed in more than 190 countries around the world, resulting in sales of close to $6 billion in 1994. Our task is to build on the traditions of quality and value, to provide brands, products, financial results and management performance that meet the interest of our shareholders, consumers, employees and suppliers in the communities in which we operate."[25]

"The combined companies will experience economies of scale in every aspect of our business," John Brock predicted. "From sales, to marketing, to administration. We'll also achieve enhanced marketplace opportunities in every class of trade in which we deal."[26]

The new organization will also have important new international opportunities. Dominic Cadbury predicts that Dr Pepper will achieve significant results in markets outside the United States.

"It would be extraordinary to me if the Dr Pepper brand and the taste were not capable of transfer to some other markets. I think Cadbury Schweppes is very well positioned to try that out, because we have access to most markets of significance around the world. We either have our own bottling operations or we have existing franchise arrangements. In the relatively near future we will test Dr Pepper in some of those markets.

"Some of the markets to try early on would be Mexico, where the Schweppes brands already exist and where we have a significant resource, because we have made significant investments in Mexico already with mineral water and with the Crush brand. We will certainly bolster the brand in the United Kingdom, where we have a very strong selling and distribution facility. ... I think the other market where the research shows a considerable enthusiasm for Dr Pepper is Southeast Asia and even China. There seems to be evidence that a fruity soft drink would do very well."[27]

Frank Swan acknowledged the international expertise of Cadbury Schweppes. "Globally, we have bottling operations or bottling partnerships in 14 countries, principally in Europe, Australia and Mexico, and we have franchises of our brands in another 77 countries throughout the world."[28]

Swan said the new company "can provide a much greater pool of talent and a much broader set of bottling arrangements than was available to the small Dr Pepper team. ... Now we can take the brand and give it access to greater critical mass and manpower resources around the world."[29]

John Albers agreed that Cadbury's strong international presence will be of great benefit. "Our international division has made significant gains, and has paved the way for making huge strides for Dr Pepper," he said. "With Cadbury now in a position to virtually explode on the international scene with Dr Pepper in a manner we never envisioned, merging with Cadbury makes growth in that area look incredibly great for the next two or three years."[30]

Shared Values

Albers said most employees seem to understand why the company was sold to Cadbury.

"The response by the bottlers was heart-warming. I had an employee say, 'Thank you for what you've done.' I think they realized that once we were able to build such a successful company, once we went public, we always had the possibility that somebody was going to come in. I think those who understand business aren't overly surprised. I think most employees feel very good they had an opportunity to work here, and many have enjoyed the benefits of being stockholders.[31]

"After two years of public trading, once we doubled the value of the stock, we were vulnerable, and there was no way we could stop it if they came in at that point."[32]

Albers spoke with fondness about the company he leaves after 25 years. "The company we put together over the years, as you know, has been the talk of the industry. In fact, it has really been the talk of the industry since Dr Pepper went private 11 years ago. What followed, the merger of the Seven-Up Company, and the public offering of our stock in 1993, ranks as one of the premier success stories in the history of the soft drink business,

Frank Swan, managing director of Cadbury Schweppes' Global Beverage Stream.

and to the best of my knowledge, in any industry in the United States."[33]

Dominic Cadbury is confident that the two companies are a good match because they share similar values and business ideals.

"My feeling at this point, right at the start of the merger, is that it's very easy coming together because you find very similar people. You find a similar atmosphere as you go around. I have sensed, even in the last two or three days, talking with investment analysts and institutions ... that we were coming up with similar sorts of answers in the sense of our approach to business. I think it is about relationships, values, approaches to business and to business relationships. They seem very, very similar to me, and I think that is what will count as the most important thing in the long term to ensure the success of the combined enterprise."[34]

Chapter I

1. Harry E. Ellis, *Dr Pepper, King of Beverages* Vol. 1 (Dallas: Dr Pepper Company, 1979), 30.
2. *Ibid.*, 29.
3. *Ibid.*, 33.
4. *Ibid.*, 34.
5. *Ibid.*, 26.
6. *Ibid.*, 26.
7. Roger Conger, "Last of the Fire–Eaters," *True West*, September-October 1962, 57.
8. Reprint of the handbill circulated by Judge Gerald.
9. "Fire–Eaters," 58.
10. Reprint of the handbill circulated by Judge Gerald.
11. "Fire–Eaters," 59.
12. *Ibid.*
13. *Ibid.*
14. *King of Beverages*, Vol. 1, 27.
15. "Gerald–Harris Street Duel," *Waco Daily Telephone*, November 19, 1897. Reprinted in "Fire– Eaters," 58.
16. "Fire–Eaters," 59.

Chapter II

1. Harry E. Ellis, Dr Pepper, *King of Beverages* Vol. 1 (Dallas: Dr Pepper Company, 1979), 23.
2. *Ibid.*, 24.
3. *Ibid.*, 13.
4. William H. McCullough, "Keeping the Record Straight. The True Story of Dr Pepper," undated, late Thirties or early Forties, 1.
5. *King of Beverages*, Vol. 1, 12.
6. *Ibid.*, 29.
7. *United States Patent Book*, 1885.
8. "The True Story," 2.
9. "Dr Pepper's Virginia Clan," letter by Jean Gillepsie Walker to the *Roanoke Times & World Report*, July 9, 1982.
10. Florence Pepper Raya, *The History of the Pepper Family in America and Allied Lines* (Fort Madison, Iowa: The Evening Democrat Company, 1974), 26.
11. Liz Gordon, "The Friendly Pepper–Upper," *Texas Highways*, July 1993, 39.
12. *History of the Pepper Family*, 30.
13. "The True Story," 2.
14.. Milly Walker, interviewed by Karen Nitkin, June 5, 1995.
15. Charles Grier, interviewed by the author, December 5, 1994, St. Louis, Missouri. Transcript, 4.
16. *King of Beverages*, Vol. 1, 109.
17. *Ibid.*
18. *Ibid.*, 101.
19. *Ibid.*, 17.

Chapter III

1. Letter from Milly Walker to the author, April 19, 1995.
2. Harry E. Ellis, Dr Pepper, *King of Beverages* Vol. 1 (Dallas: Dr Pepper Company, 1979), 30.
3. Walker, letter to the author, April 19, 1995.
4. Charles Grier, interviewed by the author, December 5, 1994, St. Louis, Missouri. Transcript, 27–28.
5. Jim Ball, interviewed by the author, November 22, 1994, Dallas, Texas. Transcript, 34.
6. Grier interview, 19.
7. "Dr Pepper Complete Newspaper Proofs," published by Dr Pepper, bound volume, 1927.
8. Woodrow Wilson "Foots" Clements, interviewed by the author, November 21, 1994, Dallas, Texas. Transcript, 6.
9. Clements interview, 4.
10. "History of Carbonated Beverages," undated and unsigned, compiled for Arthur Crisp for his 1948 mural by the Dr Pepper Company, 7.
11. "History of Carbonated Beverages," 9.
12. "General Development of the Bottled Carbonated Beverage Industry in the United States," booklet, (Washington, D.C.: American Bottlers of Carbonated Beverages, April 1958).
13. Grier interview, 16.
14. *King of Beverages*, Vol. 1. 46.
15. *Ibid.*, 41.
16. *Ibid.*, 43.
17. "200 Refreshing Years. The Merry Tale of America's Sparkling Soft Drinks," pamphlet, (Washington D.C.: National Soft Drink Association, 1976).
18. Clements, interviewed for the Baylor University Institute for Oral History by Thomas Lee Charlton, April 30, 1986. Transcript, 660. Between 1984 and 1986, Clements was interviewed 13 times by Charlton or David Stricklin. Bound volumes of the transcripts from these interviews have provided valuable material for this book.
19. Daniel J. Forrestal, *The History of the Seven–Up Company*, unpublished manuscript, 1979, Chapter 1, page 4.
20. "Insidious Competition," speech prepared for the 1937 Traveling University Meetings, unsigned transcript.
21. Clements, interviewed by Thomas L. Charlton for the Baylor University Institute for Oral History, November 28, 1984. Transcript, 359–360.
22. John Albers, interviewed by the author, November 21, 1994, Dallas, Texas. Transcript, 17.
23. True Knowles, interviewed by the author, November 21, 1994, Dallas, Texas.

Transcript, 6.
24. Knowles interview, 8.
25. Harry E. Ellis, Dr Pepper, *King of Beverages* Vol. 2. (Dallas: Dr Pepper Company, 1985), 56.
26. *King of Beverages*, Vol. 1, 144.
27. *Ibid.*
28. *King of Beverages*, Vol. 2, 86.
29. Clements, interviewed by Thomas L. Charlton for the Baylor University Institute for Oral History, November 28, 1984 transcript, 329.
30. Clements, speech for the Dr Pepper Bottling Meeting, Los Angeles, October 2–4, 1983. Transcript, 3–4.
31. *King of Beverages*, Vol. 2, 56.
32. *Ibid.*
33. *Ibid.*, 57.
34. *Ibid.*
35. *Ibid.*, 49.
36. *Ibid.*, 63.
37. *Ibid.*, 65.
38. *Ibid.*, 61.
39. *Ibid.*, 78.
40. *Ibid.*, 79–80.

Chapter IV

1. Liz Gordon, "The Friendly Pepper–Upper," *Texas Highways*, July 1993, 39.
2. Woodrow Wilson "Foots" Clements, interviewed for the Baylor University Institute for Oral History by Thomas Lee Charlton, July 12, 1984. Transcript, 248.
3. Harry E. Ellis, Dr Pepper, *King of Beverages* Vol. 1 (Dallas: Dr Pepper Company, 1979), 56.
4. James C. "Jimmy" Lee Jr., interviewed by the author, November 14, 1994, Dallas, Texas. Transcript, 11.
5. *King of Beverages*, Vol. 1., 59.
6. Clements, interviewed by Thomas Charlton for the Baylor Institute for Oral History, July 12 1984. Transcript, 247.
7. Promotional booklet published by the Dr Pepper Company in the late Forties.
8. "It's Original," 43.
9. Charles Grier, interviewed by the author, December 5, 1994, St. Louis, Missouri. Transcript, 12.
10. *Ibid.*, 13.
11. *Ibid.*
12. William Kloster, interviewed by the author, February 13, 1995, Dublin, Texas. Transcript, 15.
13. Bryan Woolley, "In Dublin, They Still Make Dr Pepper the Old Fashioned Way," *Dallas Life*, September 29, 1991.
14. Kloster interview, 16.
15. *Ibid.*, 3.
16. Letter from J.B. O'Hara to Mrs. Prim, September 18, 1946.
17. Kloster interview, 3.
18. "Discussion for 1935 Bottler Group Meetings," unsigned transcript.
19. *King of Beverages*, Vol. 1, 185.
20. Clements, interviewed by Thomas Charlton for the Baylor University Institute for Oral History, June 12, 1984. Transcript, 139.
21. Clements, interviewed by Thomas Charlton for the Baylor University Institute for Oral History, June 7 1984. Transcript, 101.
22. Clements, interviewed by Thomas Charlton for the Baylor University Institute for Oral History, June 12, 1984. Transcript, 147.
23. *Ibid.*, 141.
24. *Ibid.*, 142.
25. *Ibid.*, 142.
26. Promotional booklet, published by Dr Pepper, late Forties.
27. "Dr Pepper Complete Newspaper Proofs," bound volume published by Dr Pepper, 1927.
28. Clements, interviewed by Thomas Charlton for the Baylor University Institute for Oral History, June 21, 1984. Transcript, 140.
29. Walter H. Eddy, *The Liquid Bite*. (Dallas: Dr Pepper Company, 1944), 5.

Chapter V

1. Harry E. Ellis, Dr Pepper, *King of Beverages* Vol. 1 (Dallas: Dr Pepper Company, 1979), 60.
2. Woodrow Wilson "Foots" Clements, interviewed by Thomas L. Charlton for the Baylor University Institute for Oral History, July 12, 1984. Transcript, 235.
3. *Ibid.*, 252.
4. *King of Beverages* Vol. 2,,69.
5. "History of Carbonated Beverages," undated and unsigned, compiled for Mr. Arthur Crisp by the Dr Pepper Company for his 1948 mural, 7.
6. *King of Beverages*, Vol. 1, 63.
7. Clements, interviewed by the author, November 21, 1994, Dallas, Texas. Transcript, 7.
8. Clements oral history, November 28, 1984, 351.
9. Dollie Cole, Interviewed by Karen Nitkin, March 14, 1995. Transcript, 1.
10. *Ibid.*
11. Clements, interviewed by Thomas L. Charlton for the Baylor University Institute for Oral History, November 7, 1984. Transcript, 210.
12. *Ibid.*, 261.
13. *Ibid.*, 263.
14. *Ibid.*, 315.
15. *Ibid.*, 270.
16. *Ibid.*, 273.
17. Clements, interviewed by Thomas L. Charlton for the Baylor University Institute for Oral History,

November 28, 1984. Transcript, 359.
18. *King of Beverages*, Vol. 1, 206.
19. *Ibid.*, 226.
20. William Kloster, interviewed by the author, February 13, 1995, Dublin, Texas. Transcript, 20.
21. Clements, interviewed by Thomas L. Charlton for the Baylor University Institute for Oral History, November 28, 1984. Transcript, 365.
22. Clements interview, 12–13.
23. Clements, interviewed by Thomas L. Charlton for the Baylor University Institute for Oral History, November 28, 1984. Transcript, 374.
24. Charles Grier, interviewed by the author, November 5, 1994, St. Louis, Missouri. Transcript, 7.
25. *Ibid.*, 24.
26. James H. Wade, interviewed by the author, December 5, 1994, St. Louis, Missouri. Transcript, 1.
27. Grier interview, 7.
28. *Ibid.*, 8.
29. Wade interview, 3.
30. *Ibid.*
31. *Ibid.*, 5.
32. Grier interview, 31.
33. *Ibid.*, 18.
34. *Ibid.*
35. Clements, interviewed by Thomas L. Charlton for the Baylor University Institute for Oral History, November 28, 1984. Transcript, 320.
36. *Ibid.*, 361.
37. Grier interview, 29.
38. *King of Beverages*, Vol. 1, 216.
39. Clements, interviewed by Thomas L. Charlton for the Baylor University Institute for Oral History, January 30 1985. Transcript, 437.
40. *King of Beverages*, Vol. 1, 217.
41. Clements, interviewed by Thomas L. Charlton for the Baylor University Institute for Oral History, January 30, 1985. Transcript, 437.
42. *King of Beverages*, Vol. 1, 220.
43. Clements, interviewed by Thomas L. Charlton for the Baylor University Institute for Oral History, January 30, 1985. Transcript, 438.
44. Grier interview, 36.
45. *King of Beverages*, Vol. 1, 217.
46. Clements, interviewed by Thomas L. Charlton for the Baylor University Institute for Oral History, January 30, 1985. Transcript, 426.
47. Grier interview, 34.
48. Dave Thomas, interviewed by the author, December 21, 1994. Transcript, 4.
49. Grier interview, 36.
50. *King of Beverages*, Vol. 1, 240.
51. Grier interview, 38.
52. *King of Beverages*, Vol. 1, 219.
53. *Ibid.*, 67.

Chapter VI

1. John Albers, interviewed by the author, November 21, 1994, Dallas, Texas. Transcript, 9.
2. True Knowles, interviewed by the author, November 21 1994, Dallas, Texas. Transcript, 25.
3. Woodrow Wilson "Foots" Clements, interviewed for the Baylor University Institute for Oral History by Thomas Lee Charlton, January 30 1985, Dallas, Texas. Transcript, 383.
4. *Ibid.*, 385.
5. Clements, interviewed by Thomas L. Charlton for the Baylor University Institute for Oral History, May 9, 1984. Transcript, 2.
6. *Ibid.*, 5.
7. Kent Demaret, "'Foots' Clements, Master of the Soft Drink Sell, Makes a Hot Deal." *People* magazine, September 8 1986.
8. Clements, interviewed by Thomas L. Charlton for the Baylor University Institute for Oral History, May 9, 1984. Transcript, 32.
9. Clements, interviewed by Thomas L. Charlton for the Baylor University Institute for Oral History, June 7, 1984. Transcript, 89.
10. *Ibid.*, 98.
11. Clements, interviewed by Thomas L. Charlton for the Baylor University Institute for Oral History, November 7 1984. Transcript, 288.
12. Clements, interviewed by the author, November 21, 1994, Dallas, Texas. Transcript, 19.
13. Clements, interviewed by Thomas L. Charlton for the Baylor University Institute for Oral History, January 30, 1985. Transcript, 404.
14.. Dave Thomas, interviewed by the author, December 21, 1994. Transcript, 2.
15. Harry E. Ellis, Dr Pepper, *King of Beverages* Vol. 1 (Dallas: Dr Pepper Company, 1979), 226.
16. *Ibid.*, 69.
17. John Albers, interviewed by the author, November 21, 1994, Dallas, Texas. Transcript, 12.
18. Clements, interviewed by Thomas L. Charlton for the Baylor University Institute for Oral History, January 30, 1985. Transcript, 411.
19. John Clarke, interviewed by the author, November 21, 1994, Dallas, Texas. Transcript, 7.
20. Clements, interviewed by Thomas L. Charlton

for the Baylor University Institute for Oral History, February 13, 1985. Transcript, 470.
21. *Ibid.*, 482.
22. *Ibid.*, 495.
23. *Ibid.*, 496.
24. Annual Soft Drink Report, *Beverage Industry*, March, 1995, SD5 and SD11.
25. Clarke interview, 7.
26. *Ibid.*, 6.
27. Clements, interviewed by Thomas L. Charlton for the Baylor University Institute for Oral History, January 30, 1985. Transcript, 423.
28. Clements interview, 21.
29. Clements, interviewed by Thomas L. Charlton for the Baylor University Institute for Oral History, February 20, 1985. Transcript, 530.
30. Albers interview, 28.
31. *Ibid.*, 26.
32. *Ibid.*, 28.
33. "This is Our Story," Welch Foods, Printed in USA, Fourth Edition, undated booklet, 4.
34. *Ibid.*, 6.
35. *Ibid.*, 16.
36. Mike McGrath, interviewed by the author, November 22 1994, Dallas, Texas. Transcript, 5.
37. *Ibid.*, 6.
38. Mike Galt, interviewed by Karen Nitkin, April 3, 1995.
39. Galt interview.
40. McGrath interview, 11.
41. *Ibid.*, 13.
42. Clements, interviewed by Thomas L. Charlton for the Baylor University Institute for Oral History, February 20, 1985. Transcript, 535.
43. *Ibid.*, 532.
44. Clements, interviewed by Thomas L. Charlton for the Baylor University Institute for Oral History, April 16, 1986. Transcript, 585–586.
45. Jim Ball, interviewed by the author, November 22, 1994. Dallas, Texas. Transcript, 8–9.
46. Albers interview, 33.
47. Clarke interview, 2.
48. Ira Rosenstein, interviewed by the author, February 15, 1995, Dallas, Texas. Transcript, 8.
49. *Ibid.*, 4–5.
50. Ball interview, 46.
51. *Ibid.*, 47.
52. Albers interview, 33.
53. *Ibid.*, 50.
54. Howard Rudnitsky, "Lots of Fizz." *Forbes*, August 1, 1994.
55. Albers interview, 29.
56. "Lots of Fizz."
57. Clarke interview, 9.

Chapter VII

1. Unpublished manuscript of Daniel J. Forrestal, Chapter 2, page 3. The early history of Seven–Up was carefully documented by Forrestal, former director of public relations at Monsanto Chemical Company of St. Louis, who planned to publish a history of the company in 1979, to coincide with Seven–Up's 50th anniversary. When the Phillip Morris Company acquired Seven–Up in 1978, the project was suspended, and the information is published here for the first time.
2. Harry E. Ellis, in the dedication of Forrestal's manuscript, 5E.
3. Forrestal manuscript, Chapter 2, page 5.
4. *Ibid.*, Chapter 2, page 6.
5. *Ibid.*, Chapter 2, page 7.
6. *Ibid.*, Chapter 2, page 8.
7. *Ibid.*, Chapter 2, page 12.
8. *Ibid.*, Chapter 2, page 13.
9. *Ibid.*
10. *Ibid.*, Chapter 2, page 10.
11. *Ibid.*, Chapter 2, page 15.
12. *Ibid.*, Chapter 2, page 17.
13. *Ibid.*, Chapter 3, page 1.
14. *Ibid.*, Chapter 3, page 6.
15. *Ibid.*
16. *Ibid.*, Chapter 3, page 7.

Chapter VIII

1. Daniel J. Forrestal, unpublished manuscript, Chapter 4, page 2.
2. *Ibid.*
3. *Ibid.*, Chapter 3, page 13.
4. Press release from Ben H. Wells to All Members of the Seven–Up Family, October 25, 1977.
5. Statistics from Forrestal manuscript, Chapter 1, page 4, and the "Annual Soft Drink Report," *Beverage Industry*, March 1995, SD3 and SD5.
6. Forrestal manuscript, Chapter 4, page 7.
7. *Ibid.*, Chapter 4, page 8.
8. *Ibid.*, Chapter 4, page 8.
9. Forrestal manuscript, Chapter 4, page 12.
10. *Ibid.*, Chapter 12, page 12.
11. *Ibid.*, Chapter 12, page 5.
12. *Ibid.*, Chapter 12, page 8.

Chapter IX

1. Daniel J. Forrestal, unpublished manuscript, Chapter 3, pages 24–26.
2. *Ibid.*, Chapter 3, page 22.
3. William E. Winter, interviewed by the author, December 5, 1994, St. Louis, Missouri. Transcript, 5ff.
4. *Ibid.*, 9.
5. *Ibid.*, 9–10.
6. *Ibid.*, 5–6.
7. Forrestal manuscript, Chapter 5, page 4.
8. *Ibid.*, Chapter 5, page 6.
9. *Ibid.*, Chapter 5, page 10.
10. Winter interview, 2.
11. *Ibid.*, 4.
12. Forrestal manuscript, Chapter 5, page 16ff.
13. *Ibid.*, Chapter 13, page 3.
14. *Ibid.*, Chapter 13,

page 7.
15. *Ibid.*, Chapter 6, page 5.
16. *Ibid.*, Chapter 6, page 7.
17. *Ibid.*, Chapter 7, page 6.
18. *Ibid.*
19. *Ibid.*, Chapter 7, page 16.
20. *Ibid.*, Chapter 9, page 1.
21. Winter interview, 10.
22. *Ibid.*, 5ff.
23. *Ibid.*, 8.
24. Ben Wells, Internal Memo to All Members of the Seven–Up Family, October 25, 1977.

Chapter X

1. Francis I. Mullin, interviewed by the author, November 22, 1994, Dallas, Texas. Transcript, 8.
2. William E. Winter, interviewed by the author, December 5, 1994, St. Louis, Missouri. Transcript, 42–43.
3. *Ibid.*, 43.
4. *Ibid.*, 45.
5. Daniel J. Forrestal, unpublished manuscript, Chapter 11, page 7.
6. *Beverage Industry* and John C. Maxwell Associates, as quoted in Forrestal, Chapter 11, page 16.
7. Winter interview, 21.
8. *Ibid.*, 18.
9. *Ibid.*
10. Mailgram from Winter to All 7UP Developers, May 17, 1978.
11. Winter interview, 37.
12. John Albers, interviewed by the author, November 21, 1994, Dallas, Texas. Transcript, 18.
13. "Philip Morris: Turning 7UP into the Miller of Soft Drinks," *Business Week*, April 2, 1979.
14. *Ibid.*
15. Robert Quirk, interviewed by the author, November 23, 1994, Dallas, Texas. Transcript, 6.
16. Winter interview, 19.
17. *Ibid.*, 27.
18. Mullin interview, 10.
19. "Quick Recipe Favorites, Distinctively Different with 7UP," (St. Louis, Missouri: Seven–Up Company, 1965).
20. Winter interview, 29.
21. Quirk interview, 2.
22. *Ibid.*, 7.
23. Winter interview, 23.
24. Quirk interview, 4.
25. Mullin interview, 10.
26. Marty Westerman, "What Bottlers Think of the Seven–Up Company," *Beverage World*, November, 1982.
27. Mullin interview, 3.
28. *Ibid.*, 19.

Chapter XI

1. Francis C. Brown III and Trish Hall, "Philip Morris Sells Seven–Up for $240 Million," *Wall Street Journal*, October 6, 1986.
2. Jim Ball, interviewed by the author, November 22, 1994, Dallas, Texas. Transcript, 10–11.
3. Ira Rosenstein, interviewed by the author, February 15, 1995, Dallas, Texas. Transcript, 6.
4. *Ibid.*, 7.
5. Howard Rutnitsky, "Lots of Fizz," *Forbes*, August 1, 1994.
6. Amy Dunkin with Scott Ticer, "The Uncola Company Gives Bottlers a Friendly Pepper– Upper." *Business Week*. February 8, 1988.
7. "Lots of Fizz."
8. *Beverage Industry* magazine, March 1995.
9. Rosenstein interview, 17.
10. *Ibid.*, 15.
11. Stephanie Anderson Forest, with Walecia Konrad, "A Quick Picker–Upper," *Business Week*, April 27, 1992.
12. Francis I. Mullin III, interviewed by the author, November 22, 1994, Dallas, Texas. Transcript, 28.
13. John Albers, interviewed by the author, November 21, 1994, Dallas, Texas. Transcript, 23.
14. William E. Winter, interviewed by the author, December 5, 1994, St. Louis, Missouri. Transcript, 39.
15. Jennifer Lawrence, "Seven–Up Stays 'Close to Home.'" *Advertising Age*, August 1988, 15.
16. Ball interview, 13.
17. Rosenstein interview, 22.
18. Ball interview, 13.
19. Jim Gwaltney, interviewed by the author, 23 November 1994, Dallas, Texas. Transcript, 3.
20. *Ibid.*, 4.
21. *Ibid.*, 22.
22. *Ibid.*, 5.
23. Albers, speech at the 1994 bottler meeting. Transcript, 15.
24. Rosenstein interview, 16–17.
25. Albers interview, 38.
26. Gwaltney interview, 17.
27. James C. "Jimmy" Lee Jr., interviewed by the author. Transcript, 14.
28. Mullin interview, 21.
29. True Knowles, interviewed by the author, November 21, 1994, Dallas, Texas. Transcript, 16.
30. *Ibid.*, 17.
31. "Dr Pepper Bottlers Ride the Wave of Eight Straight Sales Increase Years," *Mid–Continent Bottler*, September/October 1994, 38.
32. Rosenstein interview, 26.
33. Knowles, speech, Dr Pepper/Seven–Up bottler meeting, 1994. Transcript, 19.
34. *Beverage Industry* magazine, Beverage Marketing Corporation,

March 1995.
35. John C. Maxwell Jr., "The Maxwell Consumer Report," February 21, 1995.
36. Albers, Dr Pepper/Seven-Up bottler meeting, 1994. Transcript, 6.
37. John Clarke, interviewed by the author, November 21, 1994, Dallas, Texas. Transcript, 13.
38. *Ibid.*, 14.
39. *Ibid.*, 4.
40. "Dr Pepper Commercials to Reproduce Success of '94 Campaign," *ClockDial*, Fall 1994, 8–9.
41. "Diet Spots Continue Focus on Resemblance of Taste to Regular Dr Pepper," *ClockDial*, Fall 1994, 11.
42. Knowles interview, 9.
43. Mullin interview, 30.
44. Clarke interview, 16.
45. Mullin interview, 24.
46. Mullin interview, 25.

Chapter XII

1. John Brock, interviewed by the author, April 13, 1995. Transcript, 11.
2. Douglas A. Simmons, *Schweppes. The First 200 Years.* (London: Springwood Books, 1983), 12–13.
3. *Ibid.*, 22.
4. *Ibid.*, 30.
5. *Ibid.*, 111.
6. Brock, employee meeting, March 2 1995. Transcript, 13.
7. Dominic Cadbury, interviewed by the author, April 7, 1995. Transcript, 3.
8. *Ibid.*, 2.
9. 1993 Cadbury Schweppes *Annual Report*.
10. Frank Swan, interviewed by the author, April 24 1995. Transcript, 3.
11. Jay Palmer, "Has Cadbury Gone Crazy?" *Barron's*, November 8, 1993.
12. *Ibid.*
13. Howard Rudnitsky, "Lots of Fizz," *Forbes*, August 1, 1994.
14. Cadbury interview, 8.
15. "Has Cadbury Gone Crazy?"
16. John Albers, employee meeting, March 2, 1994. Transcript, 4.
17. Brock interview, 5.
18. *Ibid.*, 6.
19. *Ibid.*, 10.
20. *Ibid.*, 8.
21. "Has Cadbury Gone Crazy?"
22. "Annual Soft Drink Report," *Beverage Industry*, March, 1995, 32.
23. "Has Cadbury Gone Crazy?"
24. Brock interview, 11.
25. Swan, employee meeting, March 2, 1995. Transcript, 6.
26. Brock, employee meeting, March 2, 1995. Transcript, 15.
27. Cadbury interview, 4.
28. Swan, employee meeting, March 2, 1995. Transcript, 10.
29. Swan interview, 4.
30. Albers, employee meeting, March 2, 1995. Transcript, 5.
31. Albers interview, February 15, 1995, Dallas, Texas. Transcript, 31.
32. *Ibid.*
33. Albers, employee meeting, March 2, 1995. Transcript, 2.
34. Cadbury interview, 11.

Symbols

10-2-4, 47
7UP., 38, 60, 62, 79, 83, 85-89, 91-97, 99, 101-112, 114, 117, 127

A

ABC, 114
Able, Dr., 22
Acid, 27, 54, 80, 82, 87
Acquisition, 70, 72, 103, 107, 121-122
Advance Mineral Water Company, 33
Advertisements, 37-39, 46, 48, 50, 55, 87, 101, 121
Advertising, 20, 36-39, 46-51, 53, 55, 65, 69-70, 73, 76-77, 79, 86-90, 93-97, 101-103, 106, 110, 115-116, 118
Advertising, Campbell-Mithun, 76
Advertising, Early, 36-37, 87-88
Advertising, Grant, 48, 76
Advertising, New, 116
Africa, 120
Africa, South, 120
Alabama, 42, 45, 53, 65-66, 114
Alabama, University of, 66
Alaska, 95
Albany, 53
Albers, John R., 35-36, 65, 69, 71, 73-74, 76-78, 103, 106, 108-112, 115, 123, 126, 129-130
Alberto-Culver, 76
Alcohol, 21, 72, 87-89
Alderton, Charles C., 19, 21-23, 25, 27, 42
All-aspartame, 114
All-natural, 61
Almond, 105

Amber, 81-82, 85
America, 13, 33, 43, 47, 54, 69, 81, 86, 94, 104, 107, 116, 119-121, 126, 128
America, Latin, 94
America, South, 94, 120
America, United States of, 116
American, Native, 52
American Academy of Achievement, 70
American Marketing Association, 70, 110
American Mineral Water Company, 33, 41
Amicable Building, 21
Andrew, Clifford, 89
Anesthetic, 19
Anheuser-Busch, 81
Anti-cola, 101
Anti-foaming, 57, 61
Anti-trust, 109
Arkansas, 32, 65
Armstrong, Richard Q., 72-74
Army, U. S., 26-27, 37, 41, 76, 80
Aromatics, 26, 29-30
Artesia Bottling Company, 15, 30, 39
Artesian Manufacturing and Bottling Company, 25-26, 29, 31-35, 70
Asia, Southeast, 128
Aspartame, 63
Athens of Texas, 13-14
Athens, Texas, 48
Atlanta, 31, 42
Austin Avenue, 29
Australia, 119-120, 128
Ayer, N. W., 104

B

Bacon Corn Crisps, 105
Baker, George, 32
Ball, James A., III, 30, 73, 75-78, 109, 111
Ballew, W.V. "Smoke," 46, 67
Baltimore, 33
Bandstand, American, 55
Baptist Baylor University, 16
Barribal, W. H., 118
Barrick, Bill, 48
Barron's, 123, 126-128, 130
Basting Sauce, Quick, 105
Baylor University, 16, 19, 54, 65, 72, 78
Beaumont, 54
Behrens Drug Company of Waco, 27
Bell, Dr., 22
Benton & Bowles, 48
Benzoate, 61
Bert Lahr Show, The, 95
Beverage Industry, 70, 78, 108, 110, 127, 130
Beverage Industry Magazine, 78, 108, 127
Beverage World, 107-108
Beverages, 21-22, 31, 33, 37, 39, 47, 51-52, 62, 64, 71-72, 97, 119-121, 123-124, 126-128, 130
Bib-Label Lithiated Lemon-Lime Soda, 82-83
Billingsley, Hascal S., 63
Birmingham, 42, 45, 67, 114, 120
Bitters, 21, 29
Blanke, Margaret, 91
Booker, Ellis, 29
Books, Springwood, 130
Bottles, 26, 31, 33-35, 39, 43-44, 53, 57, 69, 81-83, 85-86, 95-96, 102
Bottling Plant, Dr Pepper, 44, 61
Bowdoin College, 73
Bowles, 48
Bradham, Caleb D., 31
Bramwell, 71

Brann, William Cowper, 16, 19
Brazos River, 13, 15
Breweries, 72, 81
Bridge Street, 26, 29
Bristol, 23, 25, 121
Brock, John, 119, 121, 126-128, 130
Brooklyn, 97, 119
Brunswick, 73
Bryan, Don C., 53, 55
Bryan, J. S., 53
Budget Committee, 59
Buffalo Rock Company, 43
Bull, Dr. John, 21
Business Week, 108, 110

C

Cadbury, 39, 76, 119-124, 126-131
Cadbury, Dominic, 119, 121-122, 126, 128-130
Cadbury, George, 121-122
Cadbury Jr., George, 121
Cadbury, John, 120, 122
Cadbury Beverages, 119, 121, 123-124, 126-128, 130
Cadbury Beverages, Europe, 126
Cadbury Beverages North America, 119, 121, 126, 128
Cadbury Brands, 126
Cadbury Brothers Ltd, 120
Cadbury Schweppes Annual Report, 123, 130
Caffeinated, 106, 111
Caffeine, 26, 36-38, 40, 106, 111, 117
Caffeine-free, 38, 40, 97, 106-107
California, 44, 74, 76, 82, 91, 95
California, Southern, 74
Calorie-counting, 97
Calories, 62, 87, 97

Campaigns, 47, 55, 88, 117
Canada, 58, 69-76, 89, 91, 95, 105, 120-121, 124, 127
Canada Dry, 69-76, 105, 121, 124, 127
Candy, 53, 62, 79
Caps, 32
Caramel, 59-60
Carbonation, 21, 33, 85, 87, 119
Carlton, Oswald Snider, 41-42
Carolina, North, 31, 42, 58, 68, 128
Carolina, South, 32, 42
Carson Carbonating Company of Jonesboro, 32
Carver, Charles, 13
Cassagne, Gil, 126
Castles, John W., 21
Celebrated Stomach Bitters, 21
CEOs, 33, 36, 62-63, 68, 73, 76, 92-93, 103, 109-111, 123, 126
Challenges, Early, 80
Champagne, Celery, 29
Chandler, Dr., 22
Charlotte, NC, 42
Chemistry, 26-27, 49, 54
Cherry, Diet 7UP, 110
Cherry Blossom Building, 85
Cherry Cloud Dessert, 105
Cherry 7UP, 110
Chicago, 13, 47, 75, 82, 101
China, 128
Chocolate, Milk, 123
Chocolate Drink, 127
Chocolate-flavored, 62
Chocolates, 120-121
Christmas, 66
Cinnamon, 30
Citrate, 82
Citric, 80, 82
Citrus, 27, 79
Civil War, U.S., 13, 24, 80
Clark, Dick, 55

Clarke, John, 69-70, 74, 77-78, 115-117
Classification, 58-59, 69
Clements, Woodrow Wilson "Foots," 31, 33, 37-38, 41, 43, 46-48, 53, 55-59, 61-62, 65-73, 77-78
Clicquot Club Ginger Ale, 31
ClockDial, 116
Coca, Wine, 29
Coca-Cola, 31-33, 46, 51, 57, 62, 69-70, 74, 81, 85, 94, 106, 109-110, 127
Cocaine, 21, 36
Cocktail, 105
Cocoa, 120
Coffee, 43
Cognac, 61
Coke, Diet, 63, 110
Coke, Japanese, 69
Cola, Patio Diet, 62
Cola, Pepsi, 31, 33, 47, 62, 106
Cola, Royal Crown, 62
Cola-type, 128
Colas, 31, 43, 51, 60, 94, 101, 104, 106, 115
Cole, 56, 85, 96-97, 99
Cole, Dollie, 56
Cole, Dr., 99
Cole, Dr. B. C., 85, 96-97
Cole, Edward N., 56
Colgate-Palmolive, 102
Colorado, 41
Columbia Electric Company, 80
Columbia University, 49, 80
Columbus, Georgia, 97
Commercials, 92, 102, 114, 117
Competition, 31, 46-47, 54, 69, 79-80, 85-86, 88, 110
Competitors, 47, 63, 80-81, 121
Compound Honey of Tar, 22
Concentrates, 33, 60, 123
Confectionery, 120-121, 128
Confections, 21
Conger, Roger, 19

Connally, John Jr, Texas Governor, 58
Connecticut, 126
Containers, 26, 39, 86, 93
Cooking, 105
Coolers, 46
Cooperative, Advertising, 94-95
Cordial, Blackberry, 29
Cotton Palace, 43
Country Time, 124, 127
County, Johnson, 26
County, Pulaski, 25
County, St. Louis, 96
Cream, Chocolate, 121
Crisp, Arthur, 53
Critical Mass, 36, 127, 129-130
Crush, Bill, 15-16
Crystal Light, 122, 124, 127
Cyclamates, 62, 97

D

Daily Half Dozen, 46, 67
Dallas, 27, 32, 35, 41, 48-49, 53-54, 63, 65, 70, 75-78, 108, 111, 123, 126, 128
Dallas Times Herald, 75
Daniel, 96
Dark-cherry, 105
Davis, Dr., 22
Davis, Eloise, 67
Davis, Tom, 19
Delmar Boulevard, 94
Demographics, 68
Dephlogisticated, 54
Diabetes, 87
Diabetics, 62, 97
Diet, Crystal Light, 122
Diet, Sugar Free, 97
Diet Dr Pepper, 57, 62, 114-116
Diet Dr Pepper, Reformulating, 114
Diet Seven-Up, 96-97
Diet-Rite, 62, 97
Dietetic Dr Pepper, 62

Dioxide, 54
Distinguished Salesman Award, 70
Divestitures, 54, 74-76
Divestment, 54, 75
Dobbs-Life Savers International, 73
Doc, Old, 47-49
Dominion Seven-Up Company Limited, 89
Dr Pepper, 12-78, 80-84, 86-90, 92-98, 100, 102-117, 119-120, 122-124, 126-130
Dr Pepper, Early, 25, 33, 37, 69
Dr Pepper, Hot, 58
Dr Pepper, Merging, 109, 111-112, 115, 117
Dr Pepper Bottling Company, 44, 53, 68
Dr Pepper Bottling Company of Dublin, 26, 44, 58, 61
Dr Pepper Bottling Company of Macon, 53
Dr Pepper Bottling Company of Roanoke, 68
Dr Pepper Company, 29, 31-33, 35, 37, 39, 41-42, 44-45, 47, 51, 53, 55, 58, 61, 63, 67-69, 71-74, 76, 109, 111, 115
Dr Pepper USA, 77, 126
Dr Pepper-flavored Lip Smacker, 62
Drive-in, 68
Druggists, 25
Drugstores, 21

E

Eddy, Dr. Walter H., 49
Edmonton, 89
Emerson, John, 80
Emulsions, 60
England, 21, 54, 119-120
Equal, 17, 105

Erath, Major George, 13
Expansion, International, 94
Experiment, Noble, 47
Extracts, 60, 82, 91

F

Favorites, Recipe, 105, 108
Federal Drug Administration, 63
Federal Trade Commission, 36, 107, 109, 126-127
Ferguson, Hugh, 80
Fifth Avenue, 29
First National Bank Building, 19
Flavor, 29-30, 38, 58, 61-62, 69, 71, 81-82, 85, 88, 105, 116
Florence, W. L., 48
Florida, 102, 114
Foods, General, 58
Foods, Universal, 103
Foods, Welch, 71, 78
Foran, Dick, 47
Forbes, 76-78, 130
Formulas, 21, 29
Forrestal, Dan, 85, 108
Forstmann Little, 54, 73-76, 109, 122
Forstmann, Nicholas C., 73-74
Forstmann, Theodore J., 74
Fort Worth, 15, 26, 30-31, 39, 55-56, 77
Fountain, Cadbury, 126
Fountain, Provident, 26
Fourth Street, 29
Franchising, 69, 75, 94
Franklin, Benjamin, 30, 54
Frantel, Ed, 104
Freckleater, 32
Fresh Up, 84, 87-88, 103
Fruit, 21, 29-30, 60, 69, 71, 91, 105, 120
Fruit, Sparking Grape, 120
Fry, J. S., 121

G

gallon-55, 60
Galt, Mike, 71, 78
Galveston, Texas, 21
General Electric Company, 80
Georgia, 46, 48, 53, 97, 126
Georgia Tech, 126
Gerald, Judge G. B., 13, 16-17, 19
Gettysburg, Battle of, 16
Gilbert, Emily, 39
Gillepsie, Barnes, 23
Ginger Ale, 26-27, 29, 31, 33, 39, 70, 82, 88, 119
Gladney, Frank Y., 80, 83, 85, 91, 95-96
Glasgow, 119
Glass, 82, 85, 87, 101-102, 116
Glen, Watkins, 71
Golden Plate Award, 70
Golsch, Joe, 56
Granite Building, 85
Grape Bouquet, 81
Grapefruit, 27
Grapes, 71
Gray, Max, 89
Great Depression, 82, 85
Great Southern Life Company Insurance, 42
Green, Leonard M., 54-55, 57, 63, 81-82, 85
Green, Max, 63
Grier, Charles P., 29-31, 44, 59-62
Grigg, Charles Leiper, 78-80, 82-83, 85, 87-89, 91, 96-97, 99, 103
Grigg, Hamblett Charles, 86-87, 91-93, 95-97, 99, 102
Gunfights, 13-14, 16, 18-19
Gwaltney, Jim, 111-112, 114

H

Haas, Robert J., 74, 77, 109, 122
Hall, Dallas, 27
Hangovers, 83, 87-89
Harbord Enterprises, 54, 75
Harford, James, 110
Harris, Bill A., 13, 17, 19
Harris, Jim W., 13, 17, 19
Hawaii, 44
Headquarters, New, 53, 94
Hemlock, 22
Hershey, 122, 124, 127
Hicks, Thomas O., 74, 77, 109, 122
High-fructose, 44, 61
Hires, Charles E., 31
Hogan, Ben, 44
Holder, Geoffrey, 102
Hoover, President Herbert, 47
Hope, Bob, 66
Houston, 41-42, 44-45, 59
Howdy, 78-82, 85-87, 103
Howdy Company, 80-82, 85-86
Howe, Isabella McDowell, 25
Howe, Lord, of Massachusetts, 25
Hughes, Howard, 56
Hughes, Joe, 74-76

I

IBC, 69, 71-72, 124, 126-127
Iconoclast, 13, 16
Illinois, 32-33
Independent Breweries Company of St. Louis, 72
Indianapolis, 68
Ingredients, 22, 60-61, 82-83
Internal Revenue Service, 94
Iowa, 32
Ireland, 26
Irvine, California, 109
"It Likes You," advertising, 87-88, 97

J

Jacksonville, 114
Japan, 69
Japanese, 69-70
Jarvie, Charles, 71-72, 77
Jet Pilot, 56
Johnson, Lyndon, 58-59
Jones, Melody, 73
Jones, Vess, 79
Jonesboro, Arkansas, 32
Jugs, 34
Juice, Grape, 71
Juices, Fruit, 29-30, 71, 120
Justice Department, 109

K

Kansas City, 83
Kapson Laboratories, 62
Kellogg, 102
Kiefer, Ernestine "Dolly," 82
Kilduff, Jack, 126
King of Beverages, 33, 39, 52, 64
Kingdom, United, 120, 127-128
Kirsch's Beverages Inc., 97
Kloster, Bill, 44-45, 58
Knowles, True H., 36, 65, 78, 114-116, 126
Knox-Reeves, 76
Ku Klux Klan, 66

L

Lavoister, Antoine, 54
Laxatives, 38
Lazenby, Henry, 13, 39
Lazenby, Robert S., 25-26, 29, 31, 41
Leveraged Buyout, 74
Lee, James C. "Jimmy" Jr., 42-43, 68, 114
Leigh, Janet, 56
Lemon, Bitter, 120
Lemon, Sparkling, 120
Lemon-ade, Schweppes Aerated, 119
Lemon-limes, 60

Lemonade, 71
Lemonlime, 110
Leonard, Sugar Ray, 103
Leonard, Ray Jr., 103
Lilly, Eli, 27
Lime, 82, 102, 120
Link, J. W., 42
Liquid Sunshine, 27, 38
Lithia, Aqua, 29, 82
Lithiated, 82-83
Lithium, 82, 95
Lithograph, 12, 28, 40, 52, 64
Little, William Brian, 73-74
Little Rock Bottling Company, 32
Liver Pills, 22
Logos, 47
London, 119, 121, 128, 130
Los Angeles, 43, 101
Louisiana, 32, 65
Lyons, Grace, 45

L

Marlboro, 103
Marmon, Ernest, 63
Massachusetts, 25
Maxwell, John C., Associates, 108
McArthur, Camp, 41
McCullough, William H., 21-23, 25-26, 29
McDonald's, 96, 111
Mcdowell Howe, Isabella, 25
McGrath, Mike, 71-72, 78
McNeil, Max, 63
McVey, Dolly Ann, 55-56
Means Committee, 59
Mears, Martha, 47
Medicine, 25, 27, 31, 38, 48
Memorabilia, 44
Memphis, 42
Methodist, 27, 75
Metric, 102
Mexico, 65, 128
Meyer, Garret F., 79, 82-83
Meyer, W. F., 79

Michigan, 128
Military, 41, 92, 95
Milk, 62, 68, 120, 123, 127
Miller, 103-104, 108
Miller Lite, 104
Mills, Burrus, 76
Mills, General, 76
Milwaukee, 103
Minneapolis, 76
Minnesota, 76
Minnesota, University of, 76
Missouri, University of, 80
Mississippi, 21
Missouri, 32-33, 41, 47, 79-80, 91, 108
Missouri Compromise, 80
Missouri-Kansas-Texas Railroad, 15
Mixer, 88
Mockingbird Lane, 53-54, 75, 113
Montgomery, 53
Morris, Philip, 99, 102-104, 106-111, 117
Morrison, Wade B., 21-27, 29, 32
Morrison Drug Store, 21
Mott, 124, 127
Mr. Pibb, 69-70, 111
Mullin, Francis, 101, 104, 106-108, 114, 117, 126
Multi-national, 102-103
Murals, 53-54
Muriatic Acid, 27
Museum, Dr Pepper, 12, 14-18, 20, 22-28, 30-31, 34-43, 46-48, 52, 64, 72

N

Nabisco, RJR, 73
NASCAR, 117
Nashville, 42
National Bank, 17, 19
National Guard,

Pennsylvania, 41
National Register of Historic Places, 41
Navy, U.S., 26-27
Naya, 124, 127
Nebraska, 32
Nehi Corporation of Columbus, 97
"Never Had It," advertising, 38, 106, 117
Never-Failing Wonderful Mixture, 22
New Jersey, 71
New Mexico, 65
New Orleans, 104
New York City, 21, 39, 49, 53, 66, 68-71, 73-74, 95, 101, 119, 122
New Zealand, 120
Nims, Jr, A. L., 53
Nitrous, 54
No-caffeine, 38, 106
No-Cal, 97
Non-alcoholic, 38, 71, 81, 120
Non-caloric, 97
Non-returnable, 95
Northumberland, 54

O

O'Connell, Daniel J. "Joe," 96
O'Hara, John Bernard, 41, 43, 45, 49-50, 53, 61
Ohio, 56
Oklahoma, 32, 53
Old Corner Drug Store, 13, 17-19, 21-23, 25, 27, 42
Old Court House, 80
Olive, Dr. N. A., 19
Olive Street, 85
One-liter, 102
Onomatopoeia, 121
Open-top, 46
Oral History Memoir, 78
Orange Crush, 80-81

Orange-flavored, 78-79, 81
Orange-juice, 81
Otha, George, 69
Ounce-*12*, 59, 63, 86, 93, 121
Ounce-*7*, 81-82, 85, 93
Outlaws, 13, 16
Owens-Corning Glass
 Company, 102

P

Packages, New, 95, 102
Painter, William, 33
Parker, Wesby R., 57-58, 62-63
"Part of Me," advertising, 65, 71, 114, 116
Peat, Marwick, Mitchell & Co., 63
Peggy Heads, 39
Pemberton, Dr. John S., 31
Pennsylvania, 41, 54, 68
Pens-Uncola, 102
Pensacola, 102
Pepper, Claude, Congressman, 25
Pepper, Dr. Charles Taylor, 22-25
Pepper, Isabella Howe, 25
Pepper, John, 24
Pepper, Louis Ervin, 24
Pepper, Miss, 23
Pepper Free, 38
Pepper-flavored, 62
Pepper-type, 59, 69, 127
Pepper-upper, 55
Peppers, 67
Pepsi, 31, 33, 36, 47, 51, 55, 59, 62, 77, 93, 103, 106-107, 109, 111, 114, 119, 126-128
PepsiCo, 106-107, 109, 127
Pepsi-Cola, 85, 127
Pharmacists, 21, 25, 60
Philadelphia, 31
Philip Morris Companies Inc,
 99, 102, 107
Phos-Ferrates, 39
Pillsbury, 76
Pirko, Tom, 130
Plaster, Hemlock, 22
Plasti-Shield, 102
Point-of-purchase, 87, 93
Point-of-sale, 53
POMMAC, 61-62
Pop-top, 96
Premier Beverages, 71, 127
Preservatives, 61
Priestley, Dr. Joseph, 31, 53-54
Prim, Sam Houston, 44-45
Procter & Gamble Company, 71, 115, 121, 126
Proctor, John, 26
Prohibition, 47, 69, 71-72, 81, 88-89
Promotions, 48, 72, 79, 114, 116, 127
Prostitution, 13
Prudential Insurance, 111
Prudential Securities, 111, 123
Publix, 114

Q

Quirk, Robert, 104, 108
Quotas, 51, 97

R

R. J. Reynolds Company, 121
Racey, Earle, 49
Railroad, Katy, 16
Rangers, Texas, 13
Rationing, 51, 94
Ratliff, Ed, 39
Raya, Florence Pepper, 24-25
RC Cola, 105
Recipes, 58, 105, 108
Red Arrow Laboratories, 27
Reformulated, 61, 63, 114
Reformulating, 114

Research, 21, 51, 57, 69, 96, 101, 103, 114, 128
Restaurants, 67-68, 72, 85, 116
Returnable, 69
Ridgway, Edmund G., 79-82, 85-86, 89, 91-92, 94, 96
Ridgway, Howard Eugene, 89, 92, 94, 96
Roanoke, VA., 57, 68
Robertson, Mary, 24
Rock Island, 33
Rodriguez, Chi Chi, 68
Roman Empire, 54
Rome, 37
Root Beer, 29, 31, 71-72, 82, 96, 124, 127
Root Beer, IBC, 71, 124, 127
Rosenstein, Ira, 74, 78, 109-112, 115, 126
Rotman, Harshe, 75
Round Rock, 21
Route, 27, 67, 92-93, 114
Royal Crown Cola, 62
Royal Warrants of Appointment, 120
Rubicam, 48, 69-70, 116
Rudnitsky, Howard, 78, 130
Rural Retreat, 23-25

S

Saccharin Study Labeling Act, 99
Saccharine, 62, 97
Sales, 27, 29, 37, 46-48, 51, 55, 57, 61-63, 65, 67-68, 70-72, 74, 77, 79-81, 85-88, 92-97, 99, 102-104, 106, 110-112, 114-115, 123, 126, 128
Sales, Southwest Council of, 70
Saloons, 13
San Antonio, 42
Sarsaparilla, 21
Saskatchewan, 89

Schweppe, Jean Jacob, 119-120
Schweppervescence, 121
Schweppes, 39, 76, 118-124, 126-131
Schweppes, Cadbury, 39, 76, 119, 121-123, 126-131
Schweppshire, 121
Scotland, 119
Scott, Dred, 80, 94-95
Scott, Leslie R., 94
Seagram, 89
Seattle, 82
Seven-Up, Gold, 111
Seven-Up, Merging, 112
Seven-Up, PepsiCo, 107, 109
Seven-Up Canada Limited, 89
Seven-Up Companies, 76, 109, 111, 115
Seven-Up Company, 86-87, 89, 91-92, 96, 99, 102-104, 108-110, 112, 129
Seven-Up Export Corporation, 95
Seven-Up International, 95
Seven-Up USA, 127
Shearson Lehman Brothers, 122
Shoot Out, 114
"Sign Man," advertising, 114
Simmons, Douglas A., 130
Simon, Norton, 72
Simpson, Robert W., 96
Six-Shooter Depot, 13-14
Slogans, 50, 87-88, 93, 97
Soda, Cream, 72
Soda, Grape, 71
Sodas, 63, 81, 96-97
Sodium, 82
Soft drink, 24, 29, 31, 33, 38, 46, 48-49, 51, 53-55, 57-63, 65, 69-72, 77-84, 86, 88, 91-92, 95-97, 99, 101-104, 107, 109-111, 115-116, 119-123, 126-129

Soft Drink Annual Report, 127
Southern Methodist University, 27, 75
Southwestern Advertising of Dallas, 48
Southwestern Drug Company, 27
Spanish-American War, 26-27
Sparkling Fruit Cup, 105
Sponsoring, 94, 117
Spot, 63, 103, 108, 115, 117
Spring Soda Bottle Stopper, Patent, 33
Sprite, 110-111, 114
Squibb, 73
Squirt, 105, 121, 124, 127
Stamford, 126-127
Stanford University, 76
Staunton, VA., 57
Sternkorb, Louis, 39
Stitzer, Todd, 126
Stock Exchange, Midwest, of Chicago, 47
Stock Exchange, New York, 53, 73
Stock Exchange, St. Louis, 47
Stores, 31, 67, 72, 85, 93
Strategies, 114, 117
Stream, Beverage, 129
Stream, Cadbury Beverages, 121, 123, 127, 130
Streamlining, 74, 77
Sugar, 44-45, 50-51, 53, 58-63, 68, 79-80, 82, 85-88, 90, 92-94, 97, 102-103
Sugar Free 7UP, 97, 102-103
Sugar-Free, 38, 96-97
Sugarless, 97
Sulphur, 54
Sun-drop, 124, 127-128
Sunkist, 121, 124, 127
Sunshine, 27, 38
Sutter, Ma, 21
Swan, Frank, 123, 127-130
Sweeteners, 44, 97

Sydney, 119
Syrup-manufacturing, 32
Syrups, 21, 31, 33, 39, 85

T

TAB, 62, 95-96
Tabor, John T., 96
Tatum, Doris, 54
Taylor, Edward L., 82, 85, 97
Taylor Beverages, 72
Tazewell, 23
Tennessee, 23, 32
Test-marketing, 110
Texaco, 55
Texas, 13-16, 19, 21, 23-24, 26, 32, 39, 42, 44-45, 55-56, 58, 63, 65, 70, 77, 117, 126-127
Thies, Chuck, 95
Thirteenth Street, 94
Thomas, Congressman Albert, 59
Thomas, Dave, 62, 68, 78
Thomas, Virginia, 70
Thompson, J. Walter Co., 93, 100-101, 103-104
Thornton Canning Company, 95
Thul, Joseph M., 96
Tokyo, 69
Toronto, 89
Tracy-Locke-Dawson, 48-49
Train Crash, The, 15
Traveling College of Knowledge, 67
Trevino, Lee, 68
True West, 17
Tulsa, 53
Turkish Delight, 121
Tuscaloosa, 67

U

U. S. Patent Office, 22
Uncle Sam, 93

Uncola, The, 100-105, 107, 109, 115, 117
Uncola Nut, 102
University of Texas, 21, 63
University of Virginia, 25
University of Wisconsin, 89
USA Today, 110

V

Vancouver, 89
Vending, 51, 57, 95, 114
Victoria, Queen, 120
Vitamin B-1, 37
Vitamin D, 27
Vitamins, 27, 37, 49

W

Waco Daily Telephone, 13, 19
Waco Times Herald, 17
Waco Young Men, 32
Wade, James H., 59
Walker, Jean Gillepsie, 23
Walker, Lillie E., 21
Walker, Mildred, 26
Wall Street, 115
Walnut Hill Lane, 54, 75, 111, 113
Warner Lambert, 102
Warner-Jenkinson Company of St. Louis, 79, 82-83, 93, 99, 103
Washington University, 87
Water, Impregnating, 54
Water, Seltzer, 120
Water, Soda, 39, 119
Wayne, John, 56
Welch, Charles, 71
Welch, Dr. Thomas Bramwell, 71
Welch Foods Company, 71
Wells, Ben H., 83, 91-92, 94-96, 99
Wells, Katherine, 92, 95
Wendy's, 62, 68

West, J. M., 42
West, Wesley W., 42
West Indies, 120
West Virginia, 68
Westerman, Marty, 108
White House, 65
Wholesalers, 79
Windham Springs, 65
Winnipeg, 89
Winter, William E., 29, 91-94, 96-97, 99, 101-106, 108, 111
Wisconsin, 89, 103
World War II, 50-51, 53, 55, 88, 90, 92-93
Wytheville, 23

Y

"You Like It," advertising, 87-88, 97
Young, C. T., 32
Young Men's League, 24, 30, 32

Z

Zapata International, 76
Zorro, 95
Zu Zu Ginger Ale, 29